COYKENDALL'S SECOND SPORTING COLLECTIBLES PRICE GUIDE

RALF COYKENDALL, JR.

LYONS & BURFORD, PUBLISHERS

Printed in the United States of America

10 9 8 7 6 5 4 3 2 1

Library of Congress Cataloging-in-Publication Data

Coykendall, Ralf W. (Ralf Wales), 1929–
 [Second sporting collectibles price guide]
 Coykendall's second sporting collectibles price guide / Ralf Coykendall, Jr.
  p.   cm.
 Includes index.
 ISBN 1-55821-177-2
  1. Hunting — Collectibles — United States — Catalogs. I. Title. II. Title:
Second sporting collectibles price guide.
NK6077.5.C69 1993   92-35233
799' .075 — dc20   CIP

DEDICATION

My last Price Guide was appropriately dedicated to my five children and—some might think—this should therefore be for my grandchildren, but they must wait. This book is for a handful of wonderful individuals who give meaning to life.

It is for Ed Zern and Gene Hill, who walked around the corner of a big white church together and made me cry: for Ken Callahan, who visited when others chose to stay away: and for Pete Gerquest and Bud Thomas, who gave a damn.

There are other names that could be listed here—names from here and now and others from a farther place—but all share a common thread of warmth and, as you rush to this or that acquisition, I trust you will remember that the things that really matter cannot be put on a shelf.

—Ralf Coykendall
Vermont, 1992

CONTENTS

ACKNOWLEDGMENTS

As usual there are a number of people to thank for making this second book in a projected series possible — none nearly as important as the readers and reviewers who made the initial volume a success. And so to those who read the book critically and found it worthy and those who purchased it with their hard-earned dollars — thank you. You are the reasons I am back asking for your continued support with this all-new offering.

No book is the work of a single individual and I am therefore indebted to the many who helped me put all this together. My sincere thank yous go to Judith Bowman, Ken Callahan, Hank Siegel, Bob and Beverly Strauss, Bob Hanafee, Skip Woodruff, Greg Hamilton, Bob Lang, Steve O'Brien, Henry Fleckenstein, Lou Razek, David Boshart, Michael Jaffee, Janie Adams, and all the others who helped.

INTRODUCTION

The late Colonel H.P. Sheldon wrote two stories in his grand Tranquility books that seem to apply to this continuing series of sporting collectible price guides: *One To Get Ready* and *And Two To Go*. My first *Price Guide* introduced you to myriad antiques and sporting collectibles and this volume fills in a great many of the gaps.

All of the hundreds and hundreds of entries in this second *Price Guide* are new, nothing has been repeated. Some sections cover things not touched upon in the first book while others add to the depth of that earlier coverage. And — in respectful disagreement with Sheldon — I believe the proper terminology is *one to get ready, two to get set, and three to go*. In this series there will never be a definitive time to go. Each volume builds on the others and — in combination — will help you get *ready* and *set* to face the overcrowded sporting collectibles marketplace, but no book or series of books has all the answers. Nowhere will you find the information as easily as you will in my two books, nor is there a source that combines all these sporting antique and collectible treasures as successfully. But it is incomplete. There are those who know more about each of these many interests than I do, and if you have a special interest they will help if you ask. I have listed them in the appendix for your convenience. Don't get me wrong. This is a damn fine book and — coupled with my first *Price Guide*, which is still in print and available from your bookseller or the publisher — is all the information you will ever need. In spite of this I am already planning the third volume and when it's ready you'll need that one too.

WILDFOWL DECOYS

If you read my first *Price Guide* you know a bit about the history of the folk art phenomenon we know as wildfowl decoys. If you have not read the book — or another like it — I suggest you do. I know of no other sporting antique or collectible that has caught the fancy of collectors and investors as have these native carvings and no one should approach the subject without a good deal of knowledge and preparation. Decoys were first auctioned as such only twenty-five years ago, but in that short span of time their cost has risen from hundreds to many thousands of dollars, and while we may wait some time for another quarter-of-a-million dollar bird to come to market, sales continue strong and five-figure decoy sales have become quite commonplace. When one deals with that kind of money one should heed the timeless "Caveat emptor," and then some.

I was going to keep my recent unhappy experience with a *fine decoy by a well-known maker* to myself, but decided to share the details with you here, not to protect you, for I doubt that is possible when the workmanship is nearly perfect, but to prove that even the best of us can be taken in.

Last fall I "stole" an exceptional bird from a Vermont antique shop, secure in the knowledge that I had a bargain. I immediately sent the decoy to a leading auction gallery for an upcoming sale. The decoy was carefully examined and even X-rayed and — having passed all the tests — photographed and cataloged for sale at a price thousands more than I had invested. To say that I was pleased would be a gross understatement. Unfortunately the story ends on a sour note. The decoy was "withdrawn" from the auction when it was learned that it had been "reworked" and "repainted" albeit by a respected restorer. The auctioneer wisely cut his losses and the decoy I "stole" sits here and laughs at me.

There are dozens upon dozens of stories like mine told by unsuspecting decoy buyers throughout the United States, and many go back a good many years. In the early 1960s a man who is still considered to be above such things was making and selling "Ben Holmes" black duck decoys in Connecticut. In the early 1970s I spoke with a West Coast collector who had recently purchased a pair of "Shang Wheeler bluebills" for $1,800 only to learn that they were brand-new. Sad to report—these are not isolated episodes, but everyday occurrences which continue. When decoys started to fetch big bucks the reproductions just got better as the time spent producing them was well rewarded. If you are considering purchasing one or more decoys be careful who you deal with and ask for and get written guarantees unless, of course, you too want a decoy that sits and laughs at your folly.

The following prices are from 1991 and 1992 and I am indebted to Gary Guyette, Frank Schmidt, and Richard Oliver for sharing them with me. The pictures accompanying this section were taken by David Allen for Richard Oliver. The decoys are listed alphabetically by maker and/or manufacturer and the prices given are the "hammer price" and do not include the 10 percent buyers charge, which was applied in all instances.

ANDERSON, ANDY: CHILLICOTHE, ILLINOIS

Canvasback Drake: Original paint and only minor
wear. One slight crack 450.00

ANGER, KEN: DUNNEVILLE, ONTARIO

Mallard pair: Original paint showing light wear.
Hen lightly hit by shot 2,050.00

Black duck: Mint original paint and signed on the
bottom 900.00

Hen canvasback: Nearly all the paint is missing 300.00

Black duck: Original paint covered with a coat of
varnish 535.00

Blue-wing teal pair: Fine original paint with only
minor wear 1,750.00

Canvasback pair: Fine original paint; each has
hairline crack on underside 2,750.00

ANIMAL TRAP DECOY COMPANY: Lititz, Pennsylvania

Canada geese: Carton of six in their original box
with various head positions. Papier mâché 200.00

BALDWIN, WILLARD C.: Stratford, Connecticut

Black duck: Original paint. Small chip in neck filler . .   550.00

BARBER, JOEL: Wilton, Connecticut

Black duck "sleeper": Exceptional oversize decoy in
original paint with small dents in balsa body 3,400.00

Note: This exact decoy was made by Barber for my father in 1935
and has been in the family for many years.

BARNES, SAMUEL T.: Harve De Grace, Maryland

Canvasback drake: Fine original paint with only
minor defects. Circa 1910 . . . .   900.00

Bluebill drake: Original paint with minor wear and a
crack at the neck 300.00

BIRCH, CHARLES: Willis Wharf, Virginia

Bluebill drake: Oversized example with original
paint and moderate repaint 500.00

Another: Standard size decoy with original paint and
light wear 950.00

Canada goose: Solid body with old repaint removed . 900.00

Another: Repainted in Birch's style 800.00

Canvasback drake: Original paint with old shot
marks 3,500.00

BLAIR, JOHN: PHILADELPHIA, PENNSYLVANIA

Blue-wing teal: Dry original old paint and
exceptional structural condition 7,500.00

BLISS, ROSWELL: STRATFORD, CONNECTICUT

Bluebill hen: A mint decoy branded with Bliss'
brand 100.00

Bufflehead pair: Both birds are in near mint
condition and signed 500.00

BOWMAN, WILLIAM: LAWRENCE, NEW YORK

Canvasback drake: Old in-use repaint, bill with
crack, neck/body seam separation 950.00

Brant: Circa 1880. Original paint. Mackey
collection stamp. Pictured in Colio book. Rare 7,500.00

Dowitcher: Winter plumage. Once in the Stoney
Brook Museum collection. Exceptional 14,000.00

BOYD, GEORGE: SEABROOK, NEW HAMPSHIRE

Black-breasted plover: Original paint with minor
wear. Lightly hit by shot 1,000.00

Yellowlegs: Exceptional original paint and minor age
splits 900.00

DELAWARE RIVER DECOYS (*from the top*) are a drake pintail and a black duck by Reg Marter, a pair of canvasback by Jess Heisler, drake broadbill by John English, and a blue-wing teal by John Blair. Photograph courtesy of Richard Oliver—Kennebunk, Maine.

Another: Fine original paint showing only minor
wear. Several small dents 1,300.00

Black duck: Oversized decoy in fine working
repaint. From the Eaton rig 700.00

Canada goose: Canvas-covered decoy in exceptional
old dry paint and only minor chips 9,500.00

BURGESS, NED: CHURCH'S ISLAND, NORTH CAROLINA

Mallard pair: Rare pair of decoys with original paint
and weights. Near mint 6,800.00

Black duck: Oversized example with original paint
and Burgess' weight 4,400.00

Canvasback hen: Oversized example in near mint
condition 1,600.00

CHAMBERS, TOM: TORONTO, ONTARIO

Redhead drake: Near mint condition with only one
hairline crack. Early 1920s 1,500.00

Canvasback drake: Chambers' "short-bodied" style.
Near mint 7,000.00

As above: Chambers' "long-bodied" style in original
paint with one tight crack at tail 3,000.00

Ringbill hen: An exceptional example of a rare
species. Minor wear on one side 1,500.00

COBB, NATHAN: COBB'S ISLAND, VIRGINIA

Brant: Rare swimming mode with the classic "V"
tail and serifed "N." Old repaint 80,000.00

Another: Standard example with some chips and old
working repaint 7,000.00

Canada goose: Rare swimming mode; carved "N" and "V" tail. Old repaint. Minor restoration 65,000.00

Black duck: Fine worn original paint. Carved "N" and sound in structure 25,000.00

MARKET TRENDS

The many, many decoys, decorative carvings, and miniatures made by the prolific Elmer A. Crowell have provided an odd but accurate barometer of values since his work was first sold at auction in the late 1960s. You might say: As goes Elmer, so goes the market. Anyway, his prices have been off for two years, but–as I write this in 1992–they are rising. Place your bets.

CROWELL, ELMER A.: EAST HARWICH, MASSACHUSETTS

Yellowlegs: Oversized carving in near-mint condition 3,150.00

Willet: Exceptional 1890s decoy in near-mint condition 20,000.00

Merganser pair: These exceptional red-breasted mergansers date to WW I. Minor repairs 17,500.00

Bluebill pair: Lowhead gunning decoys. Original paint with minor wear and dents 1,700.00

Black duck: Has rectangular brand. Dry original paint and only minor wear 3,500.00

Hooded Merganser: The only known example of this species by Crowell. Near-mint condition 14,750.00

Note: Crowell miniatures are listed in the following section of this book.

DAISY, CIGAR: CHINCOTEAGUE, VIRGINIA

Redhead pair: Near-mint decoy pair signed by the
maker 550.00

Black duck: Cork-bodied example both signed and
branded by Daisy. Near-mint 210.00

DAWSON, TUBE: PUTNAM, ILLINOIS

Mallard pair: Near-mint with no structural flaws
and slight paint fade 1,200.00

Another pair: Repainted 270.00

And another: Oversized pair from the Starr
collection in crazed original paint 1,200.00

DENNY, SAM: ALEXANDRIA BAY, NEW YORK

Black duck: Fine original paint and no structural
flaws 475.00

Redhead drake: Near-mint original paint. Old repair
to small chip. Lightly hit by shot 500.00

Bluebill pair: Comb painting on backs. Repainted
bills and lightly hit by shot 500.00

DODGE DECOY FACTORY: DETROIT, MICHIGAN

Mallard pair: Circa 1890 pair in near-mint paint
with both necks repaired 1,200.00

Pintail drake: Circa 1885 decoy. Original paint and
only minor wear 1,200.00

Mallard hen: Original paint and minor wear with
age line in back 450.00

Redhead drake: Original paint with neck filler
missing 325.00

Another: As above with old repair 500.00

DOWN EAST DECOY COMPANY: FREEPORT, MAINE

Swimming mallard: Fine original paint and no
structural flaws 225.00

Black duck: Swimming model in original paint that
is worn in places 200.00

Three decoys: Two Black ducks and a mallard with
worn original paint 425.00

FACTORY DECOY GUIDE

*I don't know if I am supposed to tell you this yet, but Henry A.
Fleckenstein, Jr. is revising his excellent book* American Factory
Decoys, *and you should own it. No ifs, buts, or anything else. Day
in and day out, this is the most useful decoy book ever published.*

ELLISTON, ROBERT: BUREAU, ILLINOIS

Bluebill: Circa 1880 "round-bodied style" in
near-mint condition 14,000.00

Redhead drake: Rare decoy in original paint with
minor shrinkage. Fine patina 13,000.00

Mallard drake: "Round-bodied style" dating to
1880. Exceptional paint detail 22,500.00

ENGLISH, JOHN: FLORENCE, NEW JERSEY

Black duck: A fine 1880s decoy with minor
touch-up to head paint 5,000.00

Another: As above. Repainted 1,300.00

Pintail hen: Original paint with moderate touch-up.
Minor cracks 1,500.00

GELSTON, THOMAS: QUOGUE, NEW YORK

Yellowlegs: Running style with original worn paint . . 850.00

Yellowlegs: Feeding position with original paint and
some touch-up and wear 2,750.00

Dowitcher: Original crazed paint and the original bill 1,500.00

GRAVES, BERT: PEORIA, ILLINOIS

Mallard hen: Preening style in outstanding
near-mint condition 15,000.00

Mallard pair: Fine original paint by Millie Graves
covered with a coat of shellac 2,000.00

ILLINOIS RIVER DECOYS (*from the top*) include two canvasback drakes by Bert Graves, a pair of mallards by Graves, a canvasback hen by the same maker, a pintail drake by Charles Perdew, and a hen mallard sleeper and a drake green-wing teal by Robert Elliston. Photograph courtesy of Richard Oliver—Kennebunk, Maine.

Canvasback drake: Fine painting by Catherine
Elliston with a coat of varnish 2,000.00

Mallard pair: 1930s style with painting by
Catherine Elliston. Minor cracks 3,500.00

MILES HANCOCK: Chincoteague, Virginia

Black duck: Circa 1940s. Original paint with some
wear 400.00

Canada goose: Repainted 275.00

HART, CHARLES: Gloucester, Massachusetts

Black duck: Circa 1900 decoy in near-mint original
paint with fine wing carving 3,750.00

Another: Solid body with worn paint 400.00

Another: Varnish over original paint 200.00

HERTERS DECOY FACTORY: Waseca, Minnesota

Wood duck drake: In near-mint original paint 140.00

Another: As above in mint condition 190.00

Gadwall drake: An unusual species in mint, unused
condition 170.00

Mallard pair: Circa 1948 pair of decoys in good
original paint 90.00

HOLLY, JAMES: Havre De Grace, Maryland

Canvasback drake: Old working in-use repaint 225.00

Canvasback drake: Oversized decoy with worn
original paint 375.00

NEW JERSEY DECOYS (*from the top*) brant by Birdsall Ridgeway, another by Chris Sprague, broadbill pair by Levi Rhodes Truex, and a whistler pair by Roy Maxwell. Photograph by Richard Oliver.

Brant: Old in-use repaint with original showing through 1,250.00

HOLLY, JOHN "DADDY": HAVRE DE GRACE, MARYLAND

Redhead drake: Rare circa 1870 decoy in good original paint with varnish overcoat 1,600.00

HOLMES, BEN: STRATFORD, CONNECTICUT

Bluebill: A "sleeper" stripped to the bare wood. Ex-Mackey collection 10,500.00

Black duck: Old paint appears original on head, body repaint. Mackey collection . . . . Not Sold*

Goldeneye pair: Old repaint in fine condition with minor cracks and chips 900.00

* This pleased this writer as I doubted its authenticity from the catalog photograph. See introduction to this section.

HORNER, ROWLEY: West Creek, New Jersey

Black duck: Fine dry original paint with only minor
wear 4,750.00

Brant: Excellent original condition with almost no
wear 8,500.00

Canada goose: Superb dry original paint shows
average wear. Bill restoration 4,500.00

HUDSON, IRA: Chincoteague, Virginia

Brant: Hollow carved with bold original paint,
minor flaking, and small crack in neck 3,600.00

Mallard drake: This was originally made as a music
box and later sealed. 4,000.00

Black duck: Original scratch painting in fine
condition showing moderate wear and age lines . . .   1,600.00

Canvasback drake: Repainted 450.00

Merganser hen: Original paint with moderate wear
and hairline cracks 2,000.00

Canada goose: Oversized decoy with original paint
and restoration to the bill 700.00

JESTER, DOUG: Chincoteague, Virginia

Merganser hen: Original paint with only average
wear. Old filler 950.00

Pintail pair: Outstanding decoys. Near-mint
condition. Roy Bull collection 10,500.00

Brant: One of the rarest (species) of Jerter's
decoys. Original paint, minor flaking 5,500.00

REPAIRS AND RESTORATION

Repairs, restoration, and touch-up repaint are found on many fine old decoys. The question is, Who did what and how much did they do? Decoys can be enhanced or ruined by these processes and — as a buyer — you must know what, why, and who. Without this knowledge you are helpless. "Caveat emptor!"

LINCOLN, JOSEPH: ACCORD, MASSACHUSETTS

Canada goose: Classic decoy in original paint with
hairline crack 2,200.00

Black duck: Full-bodied decoy in original paint with
minor flaking and cracking 2,500.00

Ruddy duck: Rare (species) decoy in old, worn,
original paint 2,100.00

NEW ENGLAND DECOYS (*from the top*) include a Canada goose and a brant by Joseph Lincoln, surf scoter by "Shang" Wheeler, drake broadbill by Cassius Smith, and a sleeping broadbill by Albert Laing. Photograph by Richard Oliver.

MASON DECOY FACTORY: DETROIT, MICHIGAN

Mallard pair: Early "slope-breasted" premier-grade
decoys in near-mint condition 12,000.00

Pintail drake: Early "slope-breasted" premier
decoy in near-mint condition 6,000.00

Mallard pair: Premier-model decoys in near-mint
condition 8,500.00

Another pair: As above with moderate wear and
checking. One eye missing 700.00

Bluebill pair: Challenge grade with original paint
and minor wear 1,600.00

Merganser drake: Premier grade in near-mint
condition 9,000.00

Dowitcher: Circa 1915 decoy in spring plumage.
Original paint and minor wear 1,700.00

Yellowlegs: Original paint, glass eyes, and minor
wear. One age line 700.00

Note: These are the cream of the crop. Many Mason decoys are worth
far less.

MASON DECOYS including a rare drake wood duck, blue-wing teal
drake, and a scoter. Photograph by Richard Oliver.

MITCHELL, MADISON: Havre De Grace, Maryland

Pintail pair: Near-mint decoys with a minor
hairline crack in drake's neck 675.00

Black duck: Original paint with only minor wear.
One tiny crack 275.00

Bluebill drake: Near-mint with a small shot scar 300.00

Pintail hen: Original paint and minor wear. Small
checking lines in neck 225.00

NICHOL, D.K. "DAVEY": Smith's Falls, Ontario

Goldeneye pair: Good original paint. Hen has a chip
on tail 160.00

Ringbill drake: Fine detailed carving in mint
condition 250.00

Bufflehead pair: A pair of mint, unused decoys. The
drake is signed 750.00

PERDEW, CHARLES: Henry, Illinois

Pintail hen: Rare sleeping position with near-mint
original paint. Two shot marks 28,000.00

Mallard pair: Circa 1940s decoys in original paint
with no structural flaws 3,000.00

Pintail drake: Early "V" bottom decoy in
touched-up paint (white) and no flaws 2,900.00

Canvasback drake: Old repaint 375.00

PETERSON DECOY FACTORY: Detroit, Michigan

Bluebill hen: Early (circa 1880) decoy in original
paint. Minor wear 150.00

Teal hen: Circa 1880 decoy with touched-up paint
on the bill 350.00

Bluebill drake: Early decoy in near-mint condition .   1,100.00

PRATT DECOY FACTORY: JOLIET, ILLINOIS

Mallard pair: These decoys are in original paint and
each has neck repairs 240.00

Bufflehead pair: Original paint showing average
wear. Each has age splitting 220.00

SCHMIDT, BEN: DETROIT, MICHIGAN

Canvasback drake: Near-mint original paint with
hairline crack 525.00

Coot: Circa 1940 decoy in original paint with only
minor wear 900.00

Mallard drake: Signed and dated 1965 . . . .   400.00

SCHMIDT, FRANK: DETROIT, MICHIGAN

Canada goose: Fine original paint with some minor
flaking and age checks 800.00

Mallard drake: Original paint with some minor
flaking 250.00

SHOURDS, HARRY V.: TUCKERTON, NEW JERSEY

Sanderling: Rare decoy in original paint with wear.
Head has been repainted 1,125.00

Yellowlegs: Original paint with only light wear and
shrinkage . . . .   not sold*

Mallard drake: Original paint with minor wear and
age crack at neck. Rare 35,000.00

Bufflehead pair: Fine original paint. From the
Mackey collection 22,500.00

Red-breasted merganser: Fine original dry paint with
minor flaking 8,500.00

Note: As with Mason decoy listings, these are the cream of the crop
and should be viewed accordingly.

---

*NOT SOLD

*Anyone who has attended an auction or scanned an auction catalog
knows that some lots (offerings) carry an owner's reserve (minimum selling price). When the highest bid fails to reach this preset
price the item is withdrawn in a quiet and often unseen manner.
These unsold lots show up most clearly on post-auction price lists
where they cannot hide.*

STEVENS DECOY FACTORY: WEEDSPORT, NEW YORK

Redhead drake: Original paint with a few shot scars
and repaired bill 750.00

Bluebill drake: Fine original paint with shot scars
and repaired bill 700.00

Blue-winged teal drake: One of only three known.
Near-mint with "Stevens" stencil 8,250.00

Redhead drake: Rare "goiter neck" style. Paint has
been "restored" in Stevens' style 225.00

WARD BROTHERS DECOYS: CRISFIELD, MARYLAND

Canada goose: Stamped and dated (1954), this
decoy has faded paint and age checks 2,600.00

Pintail drake: 1930s decoy with old in-use repaint . 1,300.00

Pintail hen: Circa 1936 decoy with good original
paint and minor checks 10,000.00

Another: Exceptional original paint, signed and
dated 1939 . . . .   16,000.00

Canvasback drake: 1936 model stamped, dated, and
signed. Superb condition 6,700.00

Canvasback hen: Original paint with minor wear.
Late 1930s model 4,500.00

As above: Drake 4,500.00

Canada goose silhouette: Signed and dated 1952 . . .   1,400.00

WHEELER, CHAUNCY: ALEXANDRIA BAY, NEW YORK

Redhead drake: Near-mint original paint with old
repair to neck. Shot scars 850.00

Black duck: Good original paint with average wear
and minor chip 400.00

Brant: Original paint with moderate wear and
minor chipping 700.00

Bluebill: Old in-use repaint 50.00

WHELLER, CHARLES "SHANG": STRATFORD, CONNECTICUT

Canada goose: Cork and pine construction. Original
paint with minor wear 10,000.00

Black duck: Hollow pine, original paint, and glued
bill cracks 7,500.00

Bluebill drake: Exceptional paint and fine condition   14,500.00

Bluebill hen: Mate to the above. Exceptional 14,500.00

Canvasback drake: Condition as above 15,500.00

Canvasback hen: As above 15,500.00

WILDFOWLER DECOY COMPANY: Various Locations

    Mallard pair: Old Saybrook, Connecticut 625.00

    Another: Quogue, New York 360.00

    Another: Point Pleasant, New Jersey 350.00

WILSON, GUS: South Portland, Maine

    Surf scoter: A preening model with old repaint and
    minor age lines 4,250.00

    Redbreasted merganser drake: Original paint with
    fish in bill and hair crest 1,650.00

    Eider drake: Inlet head, wing carving, and original
    paint 1,100.00

FURTHER READING

There are too many decoy books and it's hard to separate the wheat from the chaff. You should read those by Joel Barber, William Mackey, Adele Earnest, and Quintina Colio for background, Henry A. Fleckenstein Jr.'s American Factory Decoys *for sure; and other regional books by Fleckenstein, Bobby Richardson, Dixon Merkt, and Charles Frank. You should also get your hands on decoy auction catalogs from the various auctioneers. It's a start.*

MINIATURE DECOYS AND DECORATIVE CARVINGS

Interest in miniature decoys and decorative carvings has grown as fast or faster than interest in decoys. Twenty-five years ago these small examples of the maker's art sold for what the market would bear, which was often only a few dollars. Today these little delights bring big bucks, with the work of carvers like Elmer Crowell, Joe Lincoln, Charles Perdew, and others approaching and topping one thousand dollars. This section of this book can only introduce this time-honored trade with pictures and prices, but if there is enough interest more will be forthcoming in a future volume.

The following miniatures and decorative carvings were sold at these prices in 1991 and 1992 and, like the other sections of this book, the list is in alphabetical order by maker. I am indebted to Henry A. Fleckenstein, Jr., Gary Guyette, Frank Schmidt, and Richard Oliver for their kind cooperation. I should note that decorative carvings are included here — not because I consider them sporting antiques or collectibles — but because they were made by decoy makers such as Elmer Crowell and the Ward brothers and are an important part of virtually all decoy auction sales.

ADAMS, FRANK: MARTHA'S VINEYARD, MASSACHUSETTS

Mallard drake: Fine original paint and Adams' paper
label 100.00

BURR, RUSS: HINGHAM, MASSACHUSETTS

Mallard drake: Excellent original condition with
Burr's stamp on bottom 375.00

MINIATURE DECOYS from Henry A. Fleckenstein's extensive collection. From the top, a hen canvasback by James T. Holly, a pair of canvasbacks by Scott Jackson, another pair by John "Daddy" Holly, and a tiny pair by the Parsons family of Oxford. All are of Maryland origin.

BOYD, GEORGE: Seabrook, New Hampshire

Canada geese pair: Controversial pair of "wrong base" decoy miniatures in fine condition 1,400.00

Canada goose: Fine original paint with minor bill flaking 900.00

COYKENDALL, RALF W. JR.: Jamaica, Vermont

Swan: Mint original paint. Signed and dated on bottom 200.00

Black duck: In "sleeper" mode. Original paint. Signed and dated 125.00

Snowy owl: Miniature perched on "dead tree" in fine original paint. Signed and dated 85.00

CROWELL, ELMER: East Harwich, Massachusetts

Black duck: Miniature with rectangular brand in fine original paint 475.00

Ruddy duck: Drake miniature with near-mint paint and structurally excellent 550.00

Canada goose: Mint condition miniature with original paper label 1,000.00

Brant: Miniature with rectangular brand. Mint 575.00

Yellowlegs: Life-size preening bird in dry original paint with minor chips 3,500.00

Golden plover: Full-size carving in original paint with blistering to one flank and leg 3,000.00

BIRDS BY ELMER

I can think of no American bird species that escaped Elmer Crowell's attention. After he stopped making decoys he commenced carving miniature game, water birds, and song-birds and sold them in sets. Crowell also sold his small carvings as decorations for desk sets, so be on the lookout for these.

HUEY, GEORGE: FRIENDSHIP, MAINE

Goldeneye drake: Miniature with fine original paint
and reglued bill 100.00

JESTER, DOUG: CHINCOTEAGUE, VIRGINIA

Merganser drake: Miniature in near-mint original
paint with minor defect on chest 1,900.00

LINCOLN, JOSEPH: ACCORD, MASSACHUSETTS

Brant: Miniature in mint original paint with no
wear 725.00

Canada goose: Miniature as above 575.00

As above: Miniature in "hissing" mode with
Lincoln's rubber stamp. Small wear at bill 1,050.00

MC GAW, BOB: HAVRE DE GRACE, MARYLAND

Canada goose: Miniature in original paint, but with
repaired neck break 400.00

Swan: Miniature in swimming mode in fine original
paint with small crack 500.00

Pintail hen: Miniature in original paint with hairline
neck crack 325.00

Bluebill pair: Miniatures in original paint and only
minor wear 300.00

Note: This pair of Bluebills was found at a flea market for $25.00

PERDEW, CHARLES: HENRY, ILLINOIS

Mallard pair: Life-like miniatures on burl base.
Near mint 2,050.00

Mallard pair: One-quarter scale pair in near-mint
condition 1,650.00

SCHMIDT, BEN: DETROIT, MICHIGAN

Mallard pair: Half-size decoratives in original paint
and signed and dated 1963 . . . . 375.00

SCHROEDER, TOM: GIBRALTER, MICHIGAN

Pintail drake: Miniature in near-mint condition with
turned head 550.00

Canvasback pair: Miniature decoys in excellent
condition. Signed and dated 1961 . . . . 900.00

Canvasback: Flying life-size drake in original paint
and fine condition. Circa 1948 . . . . 3,900.00

STERLING, LLOYD: CRISFIELD, MARYLAND

Widgeon drake: Miniature in balsa wood with
near-mint original paint 225.00

WARD BROTHERS: CRISFIELD, MARYLAND

Mallard drake: Miniature decoy in mint condition.
Rare small size 525.00

Canada goose: Miniature in original paint with
minor age shrinkage 750.00

Pintail pair: Life-size decorative birds with fine
carving and painting. Repaired by Lem Ward 10,000.00

Blue-winged teal drake: Standing life-size bird in
original paint with varnish overcoat 6,500.00

Another: Floating life-size bird with great detail and
raised wing tips. Mint 6,000.00

WILDFOWLER DECOY COMPANY: POINT PLEASANT, NEW JERSEY

Mallard pair: Original paint with no flaws. Branded
on bottom 205.00

ANTIQUE AND CLASSIC SPLIT CANE RODS

Like many sporting collectible categories — and fishing tackle collectibles in particular — split cane rods are in a slump or, as one wit observed, have taken a set that may be hard to fix. There are several reasons for this including the general state of the economy, the lack of "Eastern" buyers that disappeared with *Desert Storm* and the long-awaited slump in the Japanese economy. But the overriding current that affects all markets when it isn't ruining our casts is the omnipresent law of supply and demand. There was a time in the glorious 1980s when fishing tackle was new and exciting and money was no object. Today's buyers are few and fussy and as more and more good material comes to a waiting market only the very best gets noticed. You can thank all the publicity that we have afforded these piscatorial playthings for today's high costs and an overstocked buyer's marketplace that will probably extend well into this decade.

The following auction prices are indicative of the 1992 market and I am indebted to Bob Lang and Richard Oliver for their assistance in putting this data together.

THE 2/2 and 3/2 SOLUTIONS

I'm glad you asked. That's how beginners learn and where those "above" asking often fall on their face. 2/2 and 3/2 are two-piece and three-piece rods with two tips. If there is no such indication you must assume there is but a single tip.

The following listing is in alphabetical order by maker and the prices are for rods at auction in 1991 and 1992. The prices do not include a 10-percent buyer's fee, which was applied in all instances.

CARLSON

7' trout rod (2/2): In near-mint condition in original bag and tube 3,750.00

7 1/2' (2/2) marked "Thomas Brownstone": In revarnished but fine condition 500.00

CARPENTER

7' 9" (2/2) "Brownstone": In brand-new, unfished condition 1,200.00

DICKERSON

8' #8013 (2/2): In original bag and tube and dated 1948. Near mint 3,500.00

9' Series 85 fly rod (2/2): Has reinforced ferrules and original bag and tube 750.00

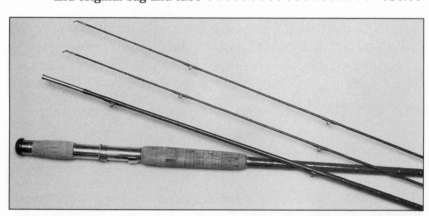

OLD DAME STODDARD three-piece, two-tip rod is ten feet in length and, in its original canvas case, sold in 1992, together with another Dame Stoddard rod of lesser importance, for $200. Photograph by Bob Lang of Raymond, Maine.

9' "Dickerson 9016 500" (2/2): With a removable
butt. Near mint with bag and tube 900.00

EDWARDS

7' Quadrate spinning rod: Excellent condition and
in the original bag and tube 150.00

7 1/2' Quadrate #40 (2/2): Has some grip soiling,
but is otherwise mint with bag and tube 1,100.00

8 1/2' Quadrate #54 (3/2): With crazed varnish, but
otherwise near-mint 400.00

9 1/2' Quadrate #25 (3/2): With only minor
problems and missing butt section 600.00

GILLUM

6 1/2' "Brush" rod (2/2): Lightly used but
near-mint condition with bag and tube 4,000.00

8' trout rod (2/2): In near mint condition with light
soiling. Bag & Tube 3,700.00

8 1/2' trout rod (2/2): In mint condition with
original bag and tube 3,600.00

GRANGER

7' "Victory" by Wright McGill (2/2): In very good
condition 575.00

9' "Delux" (3/2): In good condition with some cork
damage to handle 100.00

HARDY

7 1/2' "Marvel" (3/2): Lightweight rod in excellent
condition with bag and tube 600.00

8 1/2' "Gold Medal" rod (3/2): In very good
condition with some varnish chipping 190.00

8 1/2' "Jubilee" trout rod (3/2): Has poor varnish
that needs redoing 120.00

14' "Gold Medal" salmon rod (3/2): One ferrule
wrap gone. Otherwise very good 120.00

HEDDON

5 1/2' Musky Special: In excellent condition in
original bag 225.00

7 1/2' "Heddon #10" (2/2): One tip short and
replaced wraps 175.00

8 1/2' "Heddon Deluxe #1000" (3/2): With gold
plated hardware and walnut seat. Good condition . . .   400.00

8 1/2' "Heddon #10" (3/2): Has rewrapped guides,
but otherwise very good 75.00

9' "Heddon Black Beauty #17" (3/2): Some areas of
rough varnish and rewrapped reel seat 150.00

IS BIG TRULY BEAUTIFUL?

*Big may indeed be beautiful, but when it comes to fine split cane
rods, short is sexy. The demand for these six- to eight-foot beauties
is strong for a variety of reasons, not the least of which is that they
are fun to fish.*

KOSMIC

*8 1/2' marked "Whittemore & Co.–Boston, Mass."
(3/2)*: Both tips short and early "ring" guides 325.00

10' (3/2) marked "A.G. Spaulding": One tip short
and old "ring" guides. Very good 225.00

LEONARD

6' Model 36L with serial #1854 (2/2): The so-called "Baby Catskill" in excellent condition 2,000.00

As above repaired and refinished 500.00

6 1/2' Model 47 (Hunt) serial #8018 (3/2): In near-mint condition 2,800.00

6 1/2' Model 37-3 (2/2): In new, unfished condition with bag and tube 1,550.00

7' Model 38-H trout rod (2/2): With some minor problems 550.00

7 1/2' Model 49 (3/2): One refinished tip. In excellent condition 850.00

8' Trout rod (2/2): With "prefire markings" and in excellent condition 450.00

9' Light salmon rod (2/2): Refinished. Lacks the butt section. Very good condition 150.00

7' Spinning rod: With cracked agate guide 90.00

A LITTLE KNOWLEDGE

They say that a little knowledge is a dangerous thing, but I think none is even worse. For a brief history of rods and rod makers please refer to my first Price Guide, which is still in print and available from your bookseller.

ORVIS

6 1/2' "C.F. Orvis" (2/2): In mint condition with original bag and tube 425.00

6 1/2' Midge & Nymph trout rod (2/2): With light
handle soiling, otherwise mint 600.00

7' trout rod (2/2): In used, but very good condition,
with bag and tube 300.00

8' Limited Edition Greenheart outfit: Boxed as
issued in 1979 . . . .   850.00

8' Madison trout rod: With shortened tip in original
bag and tube 60.00

8 1/2' older rod (3/2): In excellent condition with
bag 150.00

9' Model 99 fly rod (2/1): In excellent condition with
bag and tube 100.00

9' Salmon rod (3/2): With extension butt, in
excellent condition 150.00

6' Spinning rod (2/1): In excellent condition 200.00

6 1/2' Spinning rod (2/1): Near mint 150.00

Rocky Mountain fly/spin outfit: 6 1/2' rod, two tips,
reels, etc. Mint 650.00

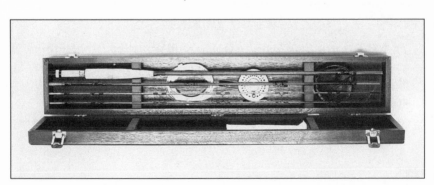

PAYNE

6 1/2' Model 96 (2/2) trout rod: in virtually new,
mint condition 5,500.00

As above: Refinished 750.00

7' Model 97 (2/2) made for A & F: In mint unused
condition 5,200.00

8' Model 102L: Originally built for Edgar Burke.
Some aging and roughness. Very good 1,750.00

8 1/2' Model 204 (3/2): Made for A & F with light
bluing. Otherwise mint 750.00

9' Trout rod: "Sold by Clapp & Treat Co." One tip
shortened. Excellent 300.00

9 1/2' Light salmon rod (2/3): With bag marks on
varnish 700.00

10' Model 216 (3/2) light salmon rod: With
extension butt for A & F. Mint in mint case 1,550.00

POWELL

7' 2" Trout Rod (2/2): In mint condition with
original bag and tube 400.00

7' 8" Trout Rod (2/2): In mint condition with
original bag and tube 400.00

7' 3"–8' 3" combination "Companion" trout rod:
With 2 butts and two tips. Mint 450.00

F. E. THOMAS

7 1/2' Special trout rod (3/2): Refinished to mint
condition. Original bag and tube 1,150.00

9' Special "Mahogany" trout rod (3/2): With one tip
shortened. Refinished 175.00

9' "Bangor Rod" (3/2): Restored 200.00

9' Brownstone Special (3/2): With one tip shortened
and the other repaired 150.00

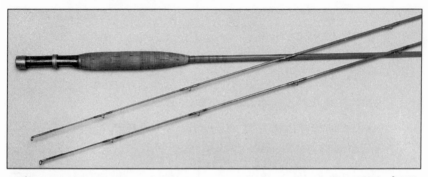

THOMAS "SPECIAL" seven-foot trout rod with two tips in excellent condition sold in 1992 for $1,500.
Photograph by Bob Lang.

WINSTON

8 1/2' Serial #6479 (2/1): Built for Hugh Balser.
Minor varnish chipping 450.00

9 1/2' (3/2) rod: Modified for tournament casting.
Owner's name and excellent condition 175.00

6' Casting rod: Good 145.00

UPRIGHT IS RIGHT

Whether you display them or store them in their cases, rods should always be kept upright to avoid sets and such.

YOUNG

7 1/2' Perfectionist trout rod (2/2): Mint, in original
bag and tube 2,500.00

9 1/2' "Florida Special" (2/2): With extension butt,
excellent condition 400.00

FISHING REELS

My first *Price Guide* introduced you to collectible fishing reels and their history dating back to the early 1880s, and I respectfully suggest you refer to that volume for that information. The book is still in print and available at your booksellers and, while it is not a monograph on this subject, beginning collectors should have this background before attempting to untangle the web of sophistry that surrounds these old and not-so-old fishing collectibles. In this volume I will try to explain the ups and mostly downs of the early 1990s, give you the reasons behind the market, and hazard a guess about the future.

As I write this we are in a "buyer's market," with many fine reels and other sporting collectibles selling below the auction estimates and prices of only a few short years ago. I gave you some of the reasons for this shrinking market in the previous chapter, and I will tell you here about the market as I see it now and in the months and years to come.

Today's low prices are the result of many things but are directly related to the "new players" who made and spent money in the 1980s as if tomorrow would never come. These "swingers" have discovered that Santa Claus and the Easter Bunny are for children and tomorrow is always just a day away. Now having heard the alarm, many of those buyers have become sellers by necessity or choice and they have flooded the market with all manner of sporting collectibles. The question is — should you buy now or wait for even better buys in the near future?

We are talking about fishing reels, but were the subject rods, flies, or glittery fish decoys my crystal ball might be clearer. Many fine reels are selling at the lowest prices in years, but Hardy reels are going for more than they did in the 1980s, so if you are looking for fine reels to use, go ahead and buy. If you are collecting for an investment I would wait and see, but watch for an upturn and jump in when it happens.

Having given you my thoughts on today's market, I am going stick my neck out and tell you what to collect for tomorrow's rewards. If you are not an angler and have taken my advice you won't be buying anything, but if you fish — and I hope you do — buy the very best reels that you will enjoy *and use*. Please notice that I have emphasized *and use*! I think today's buyers are too often concerned with investment and overlook the real reasons for the value. These fine antiques and collectibles were made to use and you will enjoy them all the more if you do just that.

The following reels are arranged in alphabetical order by maker/ manufacturer and were sold in 1992 at the prices listed plus a 10 percent buyer's fee that is not included. I am indebted to Bob Lang and Richard Oliver for their help in putting this list together and to Bob Lang for the photographs in this section.

BATE, T.H. & COMPANY

Circa 1860 marked size 4: Ball-handle reel with
wide spool and slight bend in handle 400.00

BLUEGRASS REEL WORKS

Bluegrass #3: Solid German silver jeweled model
with serial #1773 . . . .   300.00

BLUE GRASS

(see Horton)

BOGDAN

Baby Bogdan: A 2 1/4" diameter reel in new
condition with original leather case 1,300.00

As above 1,300.00

Size 00 single-action salmon reel: In used but
excellent condition 1,300.00

Number 2 Multiplying salmon reel: With only slight
wear 1,375.00

BRADFORD, MARTIN L.

Tiny (2") diameter German silver trout reel: In near
mint condition 1,100.00

CONROY, J. C. & CO

Tiny (1-5/8") diameter: Size 6 handmade brass reel
in very good condition 400.00

FOLLETT (PATENT)

Automatic trout reel: With 1889 patent date and
spring-handled operation 900.00

As above: Sample or patent model 900.00

AL FOSS

"Easy-Control 3-25": Bait casting reel in
near-excellent condition 450.00

GAYLE, GEO. W. & SON

"Intrinsic" #3: German silver with aluminum spool
end and crank. Sold by Wm. Mills and Son 700.00

HARDY

Alma (3 1/2") bait reel: German silver and
aluminum. Very good 1,250.00

Perfect (2-3/4"): With wide spool and 1906
mechanism. Very fine 550.00

Another (3"): With 1" spool 550.00

Another (2-7/8"): Mint condition 425.00

Another (4 1/4") salmon reel: Very good with case .. 575.00

St. George (2-9/16"): With agate line guide. In very
good condition 400.00

Another: (as above) 325.00

Another (3") 250.00

Another (as above) 200.00

Uniqua (2-5/8"): With adjustable drag and "Mark
II" stamping 170.00

Another (2-7/8") 100.00

Another (3-1/8") 110.00

L.R.H. Lightweight trout reel: With owner's name
and line. Very good 65.00

DON'T SCREW IT UP

*No one should even attempt to work on fine fishing reels without
the proper tools and this means without jeweler's screwdrivers.
When in doubt send it out.*

HEDDON

Model #4-15 level-wind reel: With windshield-wiper
mechanism. Excellent 750.00

Model #45 with "Carter's Patent": (1904) In
excellent condition 300.00

As above: But #40 . . . .   725.00

HORTON MANUFACTURING CO.

Meek #6: Jeweled German silver bait-casting reel.
Rare and near-mint 2,100.00

Meek #2: Very good in case 375.00

Meek #3: With minor discoloration 175.00

Meek #4: In very good condition 175.00

As above: Excellent 345.00

See also Meek

Blue Grass #7: German silver and in mint condition .   295.00

Blue Grass Simplex #25: In near-mint condition 210.00

Blue Grass Simplex #33: Near-mint 175.00

See also Blue Grass

LEONARD, H.L.

2-3/8" diameter trout reel: With the famous 1877
Philbrook patent #191813. Very good 1,000.00

2-1/8" diameter trout reel: Marked as above and in
near-mint condition 1,500.00

2-1/4" bi-metal trout reel: In "as found" condition .   1,600.00

LEONARD-MILLS marked Model 44B wide spool trout reel (*left*), and a tiny 2"-diameter William Mills & Son marked "Fairy Catskill" trout reel. Photograph by Bob Lang.

LEONARD-MILLS

Number 43 trout reel: Made for the "Baby Catskill" fly rod. Excellent 1,500.00

Model #50 trout reel: The classic narrow-spool reel. Excellent 725.00

As above: In very good condition 525.00

MEEK, B.F. & SONS

Number 44 solid German silver trout reel: In excellent condition with original box 4,500.00

Blue Grass #5: Bait casting reel. Very good 375.00

#3 Casting reel: Very good 175.00

As above: Excellent 215.00

#33 with "Carter's '05 Patent" marking 195.00

MEEK & MILAM

Number 3 German silver casting reel: With click and drag switch and ivory grasp 650.00

B. F. MEEK & SONS number 10 tarpon reel with 1902 patent date. Sold in March 1992 for $2,600. Photograph by Bob Lang.

#4 with gold click and drag switches: Ivory grasp. In very good condition 700.00

Another #3: In very good condition 450.00

As above: Showing wear 400.00

MILAM, B. C. & SON

The "Frankfort" Kentucky Reel No. 5: Marked German silver reel with jeweled bearings. Rare . . .   2,000.00

#3 with early marking 400.00

#2 in very good condition 1,000.00

#4 with ornate handle: Serial #81XX 600.00

Tiny #1 with serial #62XX: Ornate balanced handle. Rare 2,000.00

ORVIS, C.F.

C.F. Orvis marked 1874 fly reel: The early riveted
model in very good condition 425.00

Third Model fly reel: With screw construction from
Paul Young's collection 275.00

PFLUEGER

Hawkeye 2 1/2" fly reel: With January 23, 1907 and
1923 patent marking. Good condition 260.00

Golden West: With 1903 and 1907 patents, in very
good condition 250.00

Progress: With gold-plated frame. A 2 1/2" diameter
reel in excellent condition 150.00

SEAMASTER

Seamaster "S" Handle tarpon reel: In mint condition
with suede pouch 1,200.00

As above: Excellent condition 1,200.00

ORCA

*No, it's not a whale. I do crosswords too, but this ORCA is the Old
Reel Collectors Association, a non-profit group dedicated to reel
collecting. For information write to Michael E. Nogay at P.O. Box
2540, Weirton, West Virginia 26062 or call in the evening at (304)
797-1303.*

TALBOT REEL & MFG. CO.

Number 53 Four-jewel bait-casting reel: Serial
#8123. Near-mint with original box 2,100.00

TALBOT REEL & MFG CO. number 53 four-jewel reel in near mint condition with its original box. Photograph by Bob Lang.

#4 bait-casting reel: Near-mint 1,400.00

#31 bait-casting reel 250.00

Niangua bait-casting reel 900.00

As above 300.00

Another 400.00

Star marked bait-casting reel 225.00

Meteor marked bait-casting reel 200.00

VOM HOFE, EDWARD

Model 360 Perfection #3 trout reel: With Fulton St,
New York marking in original condition 3,600.00

Model 504 Tobique size 1: German silver and hard
rubber with '02 patent date 1,300.00

Model 423 Restigouche salmon reel 700.00

Another: As above 550.00

Others . . . .   500.00 to 750.00

Model 621 Ocean Reel 200.00

VOM HOFE, FREDERICK & SON

November 26, 1867 patent 3 1/2" reel: "Sets the standard for high quality reels" and near mint 1,900.00

Retail marking of Hawks & Ogilvy: This reel is much like the model above noted 1,000.00

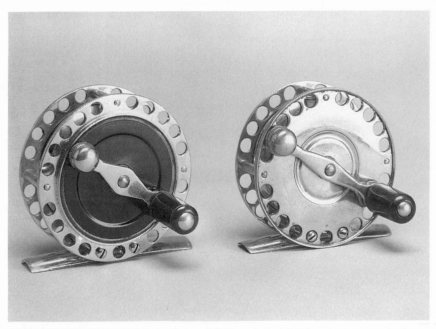

RARE JULIUS VOM HOFE REELS. A size three reel (*left*), made for A & F for only one year and a brass, perforated rim-trout reel with the "Oct 8 '89" Patent marking. Photograph by Bob Lang.

VOM HOFE, JULIUS

#3 Trout Reel: Marked with name and New York,
New York together with "real." Very good 260.00

Unmarked 3 1/2" trout reel: Good 110.00

Size 2 ball-handle reel: circa 1865 . . . .   275.00

Size 2" narrow-spool trout reel: With 1889 patent
and blued finish. Scarce 450.00

2-3/8" diameter revolving-plate-handle-trout reel:
With fine finish 300.00

Tiny #5 German silver and hard rubber trout reel: In
rare 2" size. Very good 375.00

FISH DECOYS

Those of you who read my first *Price Guide* know I openly questioned the value and validity of fish decoys as antiques and sporting collectibles of lasting value, not only at that writing, but ten years earlier as well. The following list of auction prices may well be interpreted as "proof" of either great insight or uncanny powers on the part of this writer, but sad to say, neither is true. The fish decoy market has been saturated over the past five to ten years by good *and bad* examples and as "hooked" investors now try to net a profit on their purchases they are faced with the dilemma of a poor market for a questionable product. As for tomorrow's market? I think it will be a bit like the lyrics "swim little — fiddy — swim if you can" with the poor creatures struggling against a strong tide of doubt.

The following list of selling prices is arranged in alphabetical order by maker. It should be noted that the list represents only about one half of the fish decoys offered for sale, since fully 50 percent of those that came up for bidding failed to reach their reserve (pre-set minimum selling price) and were not sold. I am indebted to Greg Hamilton of Oliver's galleries and to Bob Lang for their help with this spiny subject and to Bob Lang for the photographs included here.

BRUNING, KENNETH

> *White fish (14")*: with pearlescent hue to the bronze
> and silver finish 1,000.00

CREEK CHUB BAIT COMPANY ice fishing decoy in original marked box. Photograph by Bob Lang.

Brook trout (7"): Colorful decoy in near-mint
condition 1,700.00

Rainbow trout (12"): A yellow, orange, and white
with red fins. Letter of authentification included . . 1,100.00

CREEK CHUB BAIT COMPANY

Model 2110 Red Side Scale Fish Decoy: In the
original, marked box. Mint 1,150.00

LAKE CHAUTAUQUA

Perch (9"): Blended brown tones with maroon
stripes. Minor flaking but near-mint 3,400.00

GOULETTE, ISSAC

Brook trout (6"): With blended green and white
paint and red dots. Minor flaking 65.00

HEDDON

Bat wing ice fishing decoy: With green crackleback
finish and glass eyes. Some flaking and pitting . . . 2,250.00

PETERSON, OSCAR

Brown trout (10"): With the original "$1.25" on the
belly. Minor flaking 1,200.00

Brook trout (8-3/4"): With tack eyes and paint worn
off weights. Excellent 1,450.00

Pike (9 1/4"): With minor flaws as above 850.00

Perch (8"): An early "fat body" decoy in excellent
condition 2,250.00

Sucker (8"): With minor rubs and wear 850.00

Brown trout (7"): With finish worn off weights 775.00

Perch (5 1/2"): With one minor chip. Near-mint 850.00

Brook trout (5" to 6"): Near-mint . . . . 600.00 to 800.00

Others (6" to 9") . . . . 500.00 to 900.00

See also Peterson in Lure Section

PFLUEGER

Hard rubber spearing decoy (7"): With chips at head
and tail. Good condition 175.00

RAMEY, JESS

Brook trout (9"): With an old patch of repaint on the
belly 375.00

Brook trout (7 1/2"): With large tack eyes, metal
fins, and minor chipping 700.00

Brook trout (7 1/4"): With unusual paint pattern and moderate wear 300.00

Rainbow trout (7 1/4"): With a red stripe and black spots on a gray body 500.00

RANDALL

Six red & white 2 1/4" decoys: On original counter card in mint condition 200.00

CONTEMPORARY FISH DECOY MAKERS

These very competent carvers are not listed here. A full study of all fish decoy makers will be found in the Kimball's "The Fish Decoy" volumes I and II

COLLECTIBLE FLIES

In the first volume of *Coykendall's Sporting Collectibles Price Guide* I stuck my neck out and predicted that these bits of fluff and feathers would be the next of the many sporting antiques and collectibles to reach record heights. This has not happened yet, but the scaling ladders are out and — if the numerous auction prices I scan with great regularity are any indication — the attack is about to begin.

Flies have done exceedingly well in this time of falling prices and uncertain futures, selling for or above pre-sale auction estimates, something few other sporting collectibles have even approached. I will keep my neck out and you can decide in a few years whether you want to chop at it or call me swami.

The following flies and collections of flies are indicative of the above-noted trend. The prices were realized at auction in the recent

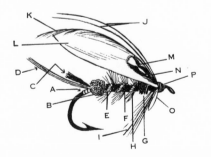

ANATOMY OF A FLY (*A*) Tip (*B*) Ruff or egg sack (*C*) Tag (*D*) Tail (*E*) Ribbing (*F*) Body (*G*) Joint (*H*) Body Hackle (*I*) Hackle (*J*) Horns (*K*) Topping (*L*) Wing (*M*) Shoulder (*N*) Cheek (*O*) Throat (*P*) Head.

past and do not include the 10 percent buyer's premium added to virtually all of the prices listed. I have avoided catalog listings of flies for sale — not because they are not worthy but because they do not necessarily represent "sold" material. A complete listing of individual flies and collectible fly-tiers can be found in the first volume of my *Price Guide*.

I am indebted to Bob Lang, Richard Oliver, and Greg Hamilton for their help in putting this material together. It is listed in alphabetical order by maker.

ARSENAULT, J. C.

Fourteen salmon flies 125.00

Another group as above 90.00

BATES, JOSEPH

Salmon fly: Matted and framed with proceeds to
American Fly Fishing Museum 400.00

Another as above 375.00

BOYD, MEGAN

Irish Hairy Mary: Salmon fly 35.00

March Brown: Salmon fly 65.00

BURKE, EDGAR

Dry fly on driftwood: In glass dome with
documentation card 300.00

DARBEE, ELSIE

Rat-Faced Mac: Dry salmon fly with letter of
documentation 175.00

DRURY, ESMOND

General Practitioner: In excellent condition 90.00

FABBENI, BRIAN

Wild Turkey: Gut-eyed salmon fly with letter of
documentation 75.00

FLICK, ART

Red Quill: Dry fly with provenance and letter of
documentation 120.00

GILLUM, PINKY

Four dry flies: Framed together with four salmon
flies by Belarmino Martinez 600.00

LEISENRING, JAMES

Set of twelve "Favorite Flies": Together with a
photograph of Leisenring and documentation . . . .   NS

MARTINEZ, BELARMINO

Roger's Fancy: Salmon fly 55.00

E.O. River: Salmon fly 70.00

See also "Gillum"

MAZZA, DEL

Display "Rise A Salmon": With fifteen flies on
driftwood. #1/12. Mint . . . .   NS

Display "Flies of Yesterday": With 24 flies on
branch. #1/10. Mint . . . .   NS

MC HAFFIE, ROBERT

Framed *"History of Fly-tying in Northern Ireland"*:
With thirteen flies. Mint 630.00

PARADICHLOROBENZENE

That's right. Paradichlorobenzene repels bugs and moths and you should use it (or camphor) to protect your expensive acquisitions.

PRYCE-TANNATT, T.E.

Salmon fly: In dome with letter of documentation . . .   250.00

Trout fly: In dome and with documentation 400.00

ROGAN, ALEX

Six salmon flies: Matted and framed with one of
Rogan's cards 325.00

STEARNS, FRANCES

Twelve "Classic Salmon Flies": Mounted and
framed. Excellent 650.00

Twelve "Irish Salmon Flies": Mounted and framed.
Excellent 700.00

Another (as above) 500.00

Twenty-five "Classic Trout Flies": Mounted and
framed. Excellent 350.00

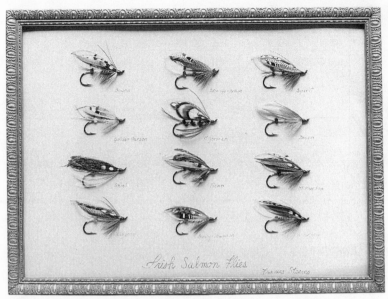

IRISH SALMON FLIES by Frances Stearns. Signed, mounted and framed. Photograph by Bob Lang.

STEVENS, CARRIE

Streamer fly "Nine-Three": Under cellophane on the original card with documentation 300.00

Eight streamer flies: Framed and with the necessary documentation by Ted Niemeyer 1,700.00

YOUNGER, JIMMY

Nine salmon flies: Matted individually and nicely framed. Excellent 130.00

COLLECTIONS OF FLIES

A & F fly box: With 275 antique/salmon and bass flies suitable for framing. Excellent 3,700.000

Four English fly boxes: With flies 375.00

THE ZERN
A FLY FOR ALL SEASONS

To celebrate Ed Zern's myriad contributions to
America's sport and humor we have taken fluff, feathers,
and some hair of the dog to create a small monument
to a big man in a limited edition.

THE ZERN is a limited edition fly by the author and fly-tier Al Bovyn
celebrating the many joys of author/cartoonist/writer, Ed Zern.

Hardy fly box and flies 70.00

Early leather fly-book: With flies 120.00

Another 300.00

Three fly boxes with flies 60.00

Boxes of fifty-year-old salmon fly dressing: Including
polar bear, seal, and bustard 3,800.00

* NS = offered but not sold.

FISHING ACCESSORIES

Anglers like gadgets. Think about it. Gunners get up, don the appropriate clothing, stuff some shells in their pocket, and go afield. The angler is undressed until he has ten or twenty pounds of this and that stuffed in his many pockets and dangling from belt and body. But this is good. It keeps all manner of oddball manufacturers in business, helps the economy, and lets me add a chapter to this book. Seriously —and believe me, the anglers I know take these things seriously— the myriad odds and ends that I have lumped together under the heading "fishing accessories" are important to angler and collector alike. Even if these collectibles are not your kettle of fish you should be aware of their increasing values. The prices listed are recent and do not include the 10 percent buyer's fee that has become the "norm" at virtually all auction sales. I am indebted to Bob Lang and Richard Oliver for the information gleaned from their catalogs and to Bob Lang for the pictures in this section. The list is in no particular order.

MEMORABILIA

Paul Young's personal fly-tying kit 275.00
Paul Young pictures, awards, etc 150.00
E.F. Payne Rod Co. record book: 1930–1964 . . . . 330.00
Letter to Jim Payne from Everett Garrison 300.00
Another from Otto Zwarg 175.00

1967 order to Payne from A & F 25.00
South Bend lure patent folders . . . . 15.00 to 35.00
Letter to Al McClane from Lyndon Johnson 110.00
Al McClane's photography file cabinet 3,500.00
McClane's personal letter file 850.00
McClane's file cabinet of correspondence 1,300.00

GAFFS, NETS, CREELS, ETC.
Marbles spring loaded gaff: Very good 150.00
86" gaff-wading staff: Excellent 100.00
Hardy gaff-wading staff: Excellent 180.00

COLLECTIBLE CREELS come in all shapes and sizes and are made of a variety of materials. Photograph by Bob Lang.

Angler's "weedwacker" made in England:

Very good 50.00

Another: as above 50.00

8 1/2' oak salmon net: Excellent 325.00

Telescoping brass and copper folding net 125.00

Adirondack 33" canoe net 200.00

Kosmic 62" signed take-apart net 55.00

Two boats nets 55.00

Two Orvis glass minnow traps 475.00

Hardy fish-handled cane 325.00

Aluminum priest: With angler's club logo 125.00

Walnut-handled priest 35.00

Two priests 75.00

Mahogany creel: With copper hinges 950.00

Carved wooden creel: With fish, flies, etc 175.00

Aluminum slant-front creel: With handpainted fish   225.00

Leather-trimmed whole willow creel 100.00

Early center-hole split creel 70.00

Squat whole willow creel: Excellent and unusual . 175.00

Dainty 5" × 6" × 6" willow creel 150.00

Tiny willow creel 90.00

Two willow creels 240.00

Two center-hole creels 220.00

BASKET FREAKS

In my first Price Guide I stated "creels are collected by fishing enthusiasts as well as basket freaks." And they are. A "reviewer" for a gun publication wrote about that first book in a way that still confuses me. My late wife and each of my daughters qualify as basket freaks *and all have used creels as pocketbooks. Perhaps when he reads this he'll write and explain his review. The fact of the matter is that creels enjoy the attention of two markets.*

FLY BOXES, FLY-TYING CHESTS AND TACKLE BOXES

Five-drawer fly chest 225.00
Twelve-drawer lift-top storage box 100.00
Salmon fly box: Three lift-out trays 150.00
Hardy four-compartment fly box 90.00
A & F tackle box 350.00
Another: As above. Early 400.00
Leather tackle box 420.00
Roll-top fly chest 450.00
Oak fly chest: With glass top 500.00
Hardy fly box by Wheatley. New. 250.00
Oak drop-front fly chest 150.00

FISH SPEARS

Spear: Spring-gaff combination 45.00
Connecticut eel spear 10.00
Seal spear 135.00
Three eel spears 285.00
Four fish spears 100.00
Two hand-wrought spears 200.00
Three hand-wrought spears 325.00

AND THE LIST GOES ON ...

Tin novelty minnow float: Rare 1,450.00
Ice saw and chisel 325.00
Edward Vom Hofe line dryer: Signed 250.00
L.T. Weiss line dryer 220.00
Royal Doulton "Gallant Fishers" bowl 300.00
As above: Smaller 50.00
As above: Plate 120.00
Miniature canvas-covered canoe (42") 1,050.00
and on and on and ...

E.C. SIMMONS HARDWARE store counter display in rare unused condition sold at auction for $325. Photograph by Bob Lang.

SPORTING ADVERTISING ENVELOPES

Sporting advertising took many appealing forms back in the good old days before the Japanese bashed Pearl Harbor and Lucky Strike green went to war. In my first *Price Guide* both calendars and posters were discussed and covered sufficiently to give readers a working sense of these rarities and their increasing values. In that first book I referred to advertising envelopes and then the subject was left hanging. This is hereby corrected and — if you are like I am — you will find these old sporting and philatelic collectibles of considerable interest. And I am sure I don't have to tell those of you who know about these things that my publisher Nick Lyons and I have adopted the Hazard Powder Company's wonderful mallard duck as our standard bearer for these *Price Guides*.

Advertising envelopes — sporting and non-sporting — came into use after the end of the Civil War and hit their full stride late in the last century when color printing became both practical and inexpensive. I am hard put to think of any major company that didn't make at least limited use of this medium and the firearms and sporting powder companies were leaders in this "free" advertising practice. In fact many of the very finest and most costly of the advertising envelopes were from sporting concerns. Companies used these envelopes for their own mailings and, most important to today's collectors, they gave them to their dealers, who in turn added their name and address and used them for their mailings. It goes without saying that were it not for the dealer of the past the collector of today would have slim pickings and only a few well-heeled investors could afford these colorful reminders of days now gone.

Now before you turn to the prices for sporting advertising envelopes — a word of warning. Many of these colorful collectibles have been reproduced. Know what you are buying and from whom you are buying it.

I am indebted to Robert Hanafee of Amherst, Massachusetts, and my Jamaica, Vermont, postmaster, Mel Twitchell, for their help in putting this section of this *Price Guide* together. Bob buys and sells these things and Mel collects them.

ADVERTISING ENVELOPES

AMERICAN POWDER MILLS

> *Dead shot falling mallard in color* 60.00

> *Another as above*: Soiled 45.00

ATLAS POWDER

> *Multicolor atlas with world* 180.00

AUSTIN CARTRIDGE COMPANY

> *Black-and-white illustration of three dogs* 120.00

BAKER GUN & FORGING COMPANY

> *Detailed illustration of shotgun*: Fine 70.00

BALLARD RIFLE

> *Line drawing of Ballard rifle*: Rare 55.00

BULLARD REPEATING ARMS COMPANY

> *Illustration of rifle and elk in brick red* 160.00

DAISY AIR RIFLES

Line drawing of "repeater": Fine 85.00

N. R. DAVIS & SONS

Sepia drawing of double-barreled hammer shotgun . . . 140.00

DU PONT POWDERS

Multicolor of champion pointer "Sioux" 45.00

1909 champion "Manitoba Rex" 55.00

Retriever with mallard 80.00

Multicolor of two dogs afield 75.00

Quail on fence post: Color 120.00

Multicolor picture of woodcock 100.00

Quail on a rock 100.00

Five mountain quail in full color 110.00

Sailors loading cannon 200.00

Pair of canvasbacks 25.000

Man stacking DuPont explosives 55.00

ELMIRA ARMS COMPANY

Hunter and dog in yellow, brown, black: Fine 160.00

FOREHAND ARMS COMPANY

Open revolver and empty shells 160.00

HERCULES POWDER COMPANY

Infallible — man in circle shooting trap 85.00

Color photograph of trap shooters 120.00

Hercules in leopard skin with club 135.00

HUNTER ARMS COMPANY

L. C. Smith shotgun with shells in sepia 150.00

Portrait of a spaniel: L.C. Smith 130.00

ITHACA GUN COMPANY

Line drawing of shotgun 150.00

Multicolor photograph of man shooting "Grand" 250.00

KING AIR RIFLES

Multicolor picture of boy in knickers 120.00

LAFLIN & RAND POWDER COMPANY

Indian shooting from back of horse: Fine 220.00

Shooter in marsh 130.00

Settler with rifle at the ready 130.00

Orange extra on flag in wreath 80.00

LEFEVER ARMS COMPANY

Line drawing of shotgun in gray 55.00

LOVELL ARMS COMPANY

Depicts factory, revolver, and shotgun 55.00

MARLIN FIREARMS COMPANY

Shows open revolver 135.00

"For Beast Or Bird" 65.00

Depicts a successful hunter 65.00

Line drawing of rifle 80.00

MIAMI POWDER COMPANY

Five flying mallards in full color: Rare 150.00

ORIENTAL POWDER MILLS

Black and gold illustration shows mallard 170.00

PARKER BROTHERS

Illustration of open shotgun in black 140.00

As above in red 120.00

Multicolor illustration of shotgun and woodcock 190.00

REPRODUCTIONS

I continue to be surprised by the seemingly unlimited number of reproductions that fool unsuspecting buyers of just about everything. Yes, there are phony advertising envelopes on the market so watch your step — at these prices caution is the byword.

PETERS CARTRIDGE COMPANY

Multicolor picture of setters on point 140.00

Multicolor illustration of hunters at rest 120.00

Another as above: Good condition 70.00

POPE MANUFACTURING COMPANY

Rifle air pistol illustration 100.00

REMINGTON ARMS COMPANY/REMINGTON UMC

Multicolor big-game rifles and elk 200.00

Shotshells, dog, and bob white quail 200.00

Multicolor of hunter with big-game rifle 300.00

"Hammerless double-barreled gun" 55.00

"Autoloading shotgun" 60.00

Hunter meeting bear on trail 85.00

Hunters climbing rocky ledge 240.00

Hawk after ducks in flight: Rare 130.00

Mountain lion in circle 65.00

Another: As above 35.00

Bear cubs with gun 45.00

ROBIN HOOD POWDER COMPANY

Robin Hood logo in black and white 95.00

Another: As above 170.00

SAVAGE ARMS COMPANY

Multicolor Indian and rifle: Soiled 140.00

Another: Light foxing 90.00

Depicts left-handed shooter: Pistol 60.00

J. STEVENS ARMS & TOOL COMPANY

Depicts factory in full color 35.00

Multicolor picture of men shooting. Camp 160.00

Multicolor of boy shooting at target 350.00

UNITED STATES CARTRIDGE COMPANY

Three "Black Shells" as triangle 35.00

Cutaway picture of "The Black Shell" 85.00

Hunter and dog at campfire in full color 160.00

FRANK WESSON

F. Wesson's Superior breech-loading rifle 240.00

As above: But depicts two rifles and shell 120.00

FOREIGN ADVERTISING ENVELOPES

Many foreign companies produced attractive advertising envelopes — Dominion, Webley & Scott, and Purdy to name a few — that are eagerly collected. They are not listed here, but don't overlook their value.

WINCHESTER REPEATING ARMS COMPANY

Two hunters and dogs in full color 25.00

Hunter on snowshoes in color: Torn 10.00

Guide pointing, hunter in foreground 75.00

Cowboy with rifle: black and sepia 120.00

Hunters with tent and campfire: Color 350.00

Winchester repeating rifles in sepia 55.00

As above: In black and white 80.00

Bear in hunter's camp 100.00

Woman hunter with brown-and-white setter 75.00

SPORTING FIREARMS

In the first issue of the *Price Guide* I covered modern sporting firearms — those made in the late 1800s or in this century and in use today — and promised to get back to you with a compilation of antique American firearms. This is that listing. Before you look at the list there are several things you should be aware of.

Rifles and shotguns are not separate headings as they were in the previous *Price Guide*. And they are listed by maker in the order they were introduced.

Handguns are not included. There are those who hunt with high-power handguns and have good reasons for considering them as sporting firearms, but I don't agree and they are not listed.

Unlike other sections of this volume and all sections in my first *Price Guide*, here I have given you two prices for each firearm listed. Old and antique firearms come in all conditions from worthless to priceless and without actually handling this or that gun it is impossible to evaluate a given example. With a price range that covers the accepted good to fine conditions, a potential buyer has something to work with, but that leaves the question of condition in their own hands and lets me off the hook. My good to fine conditions are based on the National Rifle Association's standards and every gun buyer should be aware of these guidelines before spending a dime.

NRA STANDARD CONDITIONS*

Factory new .... Just that. 100 percent in every respect.

Excellent .... All original parts; 80 percent finish; unmarred.

Fine .... All original parts; 30 percent finish; minor flaws.

Very good .... All original parts; 0—30 percent finish; flaws.

Good .... Minor replacements; pitting; rebluing; etc.

Fair .... Major replacements; cracking; bending; etc.

Poor .... Generally not collectible.

* My conditions are simplified. You should familiarize yourself with the complete NRA standards.

The following rifles and shotguns are listed alphabetically by maker with major companies first and lesser makers coming at the end.

COLT FIREARMS

First model ring-lever rifle: 1837–38. Eight-shot revolving rifle in various calibers 6,000–12,000.00

Second model ring-lever rifle: 1838–42. Not as rare as the first 5,000–12,000.00

Model 1839 carbine: 1838–42. Four variations; all are scarce 5,000–30,000.00

Model 1839 shotgun: Six-shot revolving 16-gauge cylinder. Made 1839–41 ..... 3,500–8,500.00

Model 1855 sporting rifle: Made in half- and
full-stock models. 1856-64 . . . .   2,000–6,500.00
Model 1855 carbine and musket: Revolving
five-shot cylinders (as above). 1856–64 .   2,000–10,000.00
Model 1855 revolving shotgun: 10- and
20-gauge five-shot cylinders. 1860–64 . .   1,500–5,000.00
Model 1861 special musket: 1861–65. .
58-caliber single-shot for government 750–2,500.00
Colt-Berdan single-shot rifle: Trap-door
breech rifle and carbine models. Made for
Russia 500–7,500.00
Colt-Laidley military rifle: Single-shot
breech-loading rifle. Only a few made . . .   1,500–2,500.00
Colt-Franklin military rifle: Breechloader
with gravity-feed box magazine. Rare . . .   3,500–7,500.00
Model 1878 double-barrel shotgun: 10 and 20
gauges. Exposed hammers 500–3,500.00

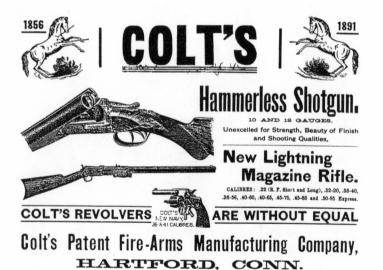

Colt double-barrel rifle: Exposed hammers,
.45–.70-caliber variations. Very rare . . 10,000–20,000.00
Model 1883 double-barrel shotgun:
Hammerless, 10 and 20 gauges. Damascus
barrels 500–3,500.00
Colt-Burgess lever-action rifle: 1883–85.
Made in both rifle and carbine. .44–.40
caliber 750–5,000.00
Lightening model slide-action rifle:

Small frame .22 caliber 250–750.00
Medium frame (various models) 350–3,500.00
Large frame (various models) 750–7,500.00

DAMASCUS BARRELS

Damascus, or twist-steel, barrels are dangerous with today's high-power shotshells and no person in his right mind should put these two together. If you are hell-bent on shooting your old Damascus-barrel shotgun, have it checked out first and then use only low-power shotshells designed for such use, such as those sold by special suppliers like New England Arms of Kittery Point, Maine.

MARLIN FIREARMS

Ballard No. 1 hunter's rifle: Made by John
M. Marlin 500–1,000.00
Ballard No. 1 1/2 hunter's rifle 500–1,250.00
Ballard No. 1 3/4 Far West hunter's rifle 250–750.00
Ballard No. 2 sporting rifle 350–750.00
Ballard No. 3 gallery rifle 350–750.00
Ballard No. 3F gallery rifle 750–1,250.00

Ballard 3 1/2 target rifle 500–1,250.00
Ballard No. 4 Perfection rifle 500–1,000.00
Ballard No. 4 1/2 mid-range rifle 750–1,500.00
As above: Model No. 4 1/2 A–1 . . . . . . 1,000–3,500.00
Ballard No. 5 Pacific rifle 2,000–4,000.00
Ballard No. 6 Schuetzen off-hand rifle . . . 1,000–3,000.00
As above: premium grade 1,500–3,500.00
Ballard No. 6 1/2 off-hand rifle 1,500–3,500.00
As above: mid-range 750–2,500.00
As above: Rigy barrel 1,500–3,500.00
Ballard No. 7 long-range rifle 1,500–4,000.00
As above: Creedmore A-1 . . . . 1,500–5,000.00
As above: long range 1,500–4,500.00
As above: extra-long-range 2,500–5,000.00
Ballard No. 8 Union Hill rifle 750–2,000.00
Ballard No. 9 Union Hill rifle 600–1,500.00
Ballard No. 10 Schuetzen junior rifle 750–2,500.00
Model 1881 lever-action rifle:

    Standard model 350–1,000.00
    Lightweight model 350–1,200.00
    Early 1881 models 750–2,000.00

Model 1888 lever-action rifle 750–1,500.00
Model 1889 lever-action rifle 250–750.00
As above: Carbine 500–1,000.00
As above: Musket 2,500–5,000.00
Model 1991 lever-action rifle:

    .22-caliber short-magazine model . . .   350–1,000.00
    .22 and .32 full-magazine model 200–500.00

Model 1892 lever-action rifle:

    .22-caliber model 150–500.00
    .32-caliber model 125–500.00

Model 1893 lever-action rifle 200–600.00
As above: Lightweight model 350–1,000.00
As above: Musket 2,500–4,500.00
Model 1894 lever-action rifle:

    Standard rifle 200–500.00
    Carbine 300–750.00
    Baby carbine 500–1,250.00
    Musket 1,500–3,500.00

Model 1895 lever-action rifle:

    Standard model 500–1,500.00
    Lightweight model 300–1,000.00
    Carbine 750–3,500.00

Model 1897 lever-action rifle:

    Standard model 150–500.00
    Bicycle rifle 500–1,500.00

Model 1897 slide-action shotgun:

    Standard model 100–350.00
    Riot gun 150–400.00

MORE MARLIN FIREARMS

More Marlin and other firearms are listed in the first edition of my Price Guide, which remains in print and is available from your bookseller or from the publisher: Lyons & Burford, 31 West 21 Street, New York, NY 10010.

REMINGTON ARMS COMPANY

Revolving percussion rifle:

.36-caliber percussion model	1,000–3,000.00
.44-caliber percussion model	1,250–3,500.00
As above: converted to metallic cartridge	750–2,500.00

Percussion contract rifle	1,000–2,000.00
Single-barrel muzzleloading shotgun	200–400.00
Remington-Beals single-shot rifle	200–400.00

Single-shot Breechloading carbine:

Type I	500–1,500.00
Type II	600–2,000.00

U.S. Navy rolling-block carbine	500–1,250.00
Model 1867 Cadet rolling-block rifle	500–1,250.00
N.Y. State contract rifles & carbines	250–750.00
Civil War musket conversions	250–1,250.00
Rolling-block military rifle & carbines	150–250.00

No. 1 rolling-block sporting rifle:

Mid-range target rifle	1,250–2,500.00
Long-range "Creedmore" rifle	750–1,750.00
Short-range rifle	750–1,500.00
Black Hills rifle	750–1,500.00
Light "Baby" carbine	500–1,200.00

No. 1 rolling-block shotgun	150–500.00
Model 1 1/2 sporting rifle	250–750.00
Model 2 sporting rifle	200–500.00
Model 4 rolling-block rifle	150–300.00
As above (Military Model No. 4-S)	500–750.00

No. 5 rolling-block rifles/carbines:

Sporting and target rifle 750–2,500.00
Model 1897 military rifle 150–500.00
As above — carbine 300–600.00

No. 6 rolling-block rifle 75–200.00
No. 6 rolling-block shotgun 75–200.00
No. 7 rifle: rolling-block action 1,000–3,000.00
Single-shot bolt-action rifle 750–1,500.00
Remington-Hepburn No. 3 Rifles:

Sporting and target model 750–2,000.00
Match rifle 750–2,000.00
Long-range Creedmore 1,750–5,000.00
Military rifle 1,250–5,000.00
Schuetzen match rifle 7,500–15,000.00

Remington-Keene bolt-action rifle:

Sporting rifle 500–1,000.00
Frontier model 1,500–3,500.00
Carbine model 1,000–2,500.00

Remington-Lee bolt-action rifles:

Model 1879 by Sharps 1,500–3,500.00
U.S. Navy Model 500–1,250.00
Military Rifle 250–750.00
Sporting rifle 500–1,000.00
Model 1882 . . . . 500–1,250.00
Model 1885 . . . . 500–1,000.00

Remington-Whitmore 1874 double-barrel:

Hammer shotgun 350–750.00
Hammer rifle/shotgun combination . 2,000–5,000.00

Model 1883 double-barrel hammer shotgun . . 250–750.00
As above: Model 1885 . . . . 250–750.00
As above: Model 1887 . . . . 250–750.00
As above: Model 1889 . . . . 250–750.00
Model 1894 Hammerless Shotgun 250–750.00
Model 1900 Hammerless Shotgun 250–750.00

Additional Remington firearms can be found in my first *Price Guide,* which is still in print and available.

BETWEEN THE LINES

Elsewhere in this volume I have told of a game of golf on an evening long ago and now, writing this cold list of firearms, I can smell gun oil and see the gleam of gun metal in the glow of winter firelight. Without these warm remembrances the listing would be colder still. I hope you never lose sight of what went into the making of the things you collect. The human factor makes it all worthwhile.

SHARPS FIREARMS

Model 1849 rifle 2,500–7,500.00
Model 1850 rifle 2,500–5,000.00
Model 1851 carbine 2,500–5,000.00
As above: rifle 1,250–2,500.00
Model 1852 slanting breech:

Standard carbine 750–2,000.00
Sporting rifle 750–1,500.00
Military models 2,000–5,000.00
Shotgun 500–1,000.00

Model 1853 "John Brown" slanting breech:

Standard model	750–2,000.00
Sporting rifle	500–1,500.00
Military model	1,500–3,500.00
Shotgun	350–1,000.00

WHO MADE WHAT?

Until 1856 Sharps Firearms were manufactured for Sharps by contract suppliers. The 1849 and 1850 models were made by A. S. Nippes of Mill Creek, Pennsylvania. The 1851, 1852, and some of the 1853 models were made by Robbins and Lawrence of Windsor, Vermont. Sharps began to manufacture guns in October 1856 with Model 1853.

Model 1855 U.S. carbine:

Standard model	1,000–3,500.00
U.S. Navy rifle	2,000–4,000.00
Sporting rifle	1,500–3,500.00

New model rifles and carbines:

1859 Model Rifle	750–2,000.00
As above: Carbine	500–2,500.00
1863 Model Rifle	750–2,000.00
As above: Carbine	500–2,500.00
1865 Model rifle	750–2,500.00
As above: carbine	750–1,750.00

New Model sporting rifles 1,000–2,500.00
New Model conversions to metallic cartridge . 500–1,500.00
New Model 1869:

    Sporting rifle 1,500–2,500.00
    Carbine 1,000–1,500.00
    Military rifle 1,250–2,500.00

Model 1870:

    Type I: percussion conversion 750–2,000.00
    Type II: early 1874-style action . . . 1,000–2,500.00
    Springfield Armory trial carbine:
    Rare 2,500–5,000.00

Model 1874 rifle:

    Sporting rifle 1,250–3,500.00
    Military rifle 750–2,000.00
    Military carbine 1,000–2,500.00
    Hunter's rifle 1,250–2,500.00
    Creedmore models 2,500–8,500.00
    Mid-range models 2,500–7,000.00
    Long-range rifles 2,500–9.000.00
    Business rifle 1,500–3,500.00
    "A" series sporting rifles 1,250–2,500.00

Model 1877 "English" rifle 5,000–12,500.00
Sharps-Borchardt Model 1878 rifle:

    Carbine 750–2,000.00
    Military rifle 750–1,500.00
    Mid-range rifle 1,500–3,500.00
    Long-range rifle 2,500–6,000.00
    Short-range rifle 1,500–3,000.00

Hunter's rifle 850–2,000.00
Business rifle 750–1,750.00
Sporting rifle 1,250–2,500.00
Express rifle 2,500–5,000.00
Officer's rifle 1,500–2,500.00

COFFEE ANYONE?

Yes, Virginia, there truly was a "Coffee Mill" Sharps carbine, but it was an addition to a Sharps carbine and not an original issue or manufacture. The "coffee mill" replaced the now famous patch box and was designed to grind coffee beans for men in the field by an enterprising New Jersey manufacturer. These devices, with removable handles, were fitted to Sharps models 1853, 1859, and 1863 Carbines, but if someone offers you one at a price you can afford I suggest you tell them you prefer tea.

STEVENS ARMS COMPANY

Old model pocket rifle* 350–500.00
Model 42 pocket rifle* 400–600.00

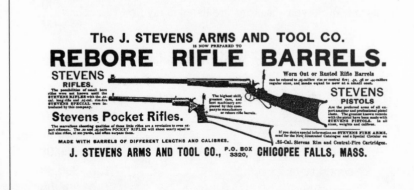

New model pocket rifle* 300–500.00
Stevens-Vernier pocket rifle* 400–600.00
New model pocket shotgun* 300–500.00
New model pocket rifle No. 40* 300–500.00
New model pocket shotgun No. 39* 300–500.00
Hunter's Pet pocket rifle No. 34* 350–600.00
As above: No. 34 1/2 . . . . 400–750.00

* Prices are for pistols complete with detachable stocks

Tip-up rifles:

Without forends 200–400.00
With forends 300–500.00

Ladies' tip-up rifles:

No. 11 . . . . 350–750.00
No. 12 . . . . 400–800.00
No. 13 . . . . 500–1,000.00
No. 14 . . . . 750–1,250.00

Tip-up shotgun 100–200.00
Removable sideplate ideal rifle 750–2,000.00
Ideal rifle No 44 . . . . 200–500.00

The balance of Stevens firearms are listed in my first *Price Guide*.

FRANK WESSON FIREARMS

Wesson two-trigger rifle:

First-type sporter 200–350.00
As above: military carbine 300–500.00
Second type 150–300.00
Third type 150–350.00

Fourth type 500–750.00
Fifth type 250–500.00

Wesson under-lever rolling-block rifles:

No 1 mid-range rifle 2,000–6,000.00
As above: Long-range 2,500–6,500.00
No 2 mid-range rifle 1,500–5,000.00
As above: Long-range 1,500–5,000.00
As above: Hunting rifle 1,500–5,000.00

Model 1862 Tip-Up pocket rifle 250–500.00
Model 1870 pocket rifle 250–500.00
Model 1870 pocket shotgun 400–600.00
Large frame 1870 pocket rifle 500–1,000.00

* Prices are for complete pistols with detachable stocks.

IS IT LEGAL?

Wesson pocket rifles and shotguns as well as those by other makers manufactured before 1898 are legal under federal law but this does not reflect state and local ordinances and it is important for you to know all these requirements before you buy any firearm. Caveat emptor is doubled when it comes to firearms and their purchase and ownership.

WHITNEY ARMS COMPANY

1798 contract muskets:

Flintlock 1,000–10,000.00
Converted to percussion 500–1,000.00

1812 contract musket:

    Flintlock 500–2,500.00
    Converted to percussion 500–900.00

1822 contract musket:

    Flintlock 750–1,250.00
    Converted to percussion 300–500.00

1841 U.S. percussion rifle 1,000–3,000.00
"Good and Serviceable Arms":*

    Maynard Tape primer 600–2,000.00
    Richmond Humback-lock type 600–2,000.00
    Enfield type 600–1,250.00
    As above: Musket 600–1,250.00
    "Mississippi"-style rifle 750–1,500.00

* These were made by Whitney from condemned and foreign parts from 1857 to 1864.

1861 Navy percussion rifle 750–2,500.00
1861 contract(s) rifle musket 500–2,500.00
Percussion shotguns:

    Double-barrel 250–500.00
    Single-barrel 250–600.00

Whitney swing-breech carbine 1,500–2,500.00
Whitney-Cochran carbine 750–1,500.00
Excelsior single-shot top-loader 500–1,000.00
Whitney-Howard lever-action single-shot 250–500.00
Whitney-Phoenix breechloader:

    Rifle 250–750.00

Military rifle 750–1,500.00
Carbine 750–1,750.00
Scheutzen rifle 750–1,500.00
Gallery rifle 350–750.00

Whitney-Laidley rolling block:

Sporting rifle 250–750.00
Creedmore rifle 750–3,500.00
Military rifle 450–900.00
Gallery rifle 250–700.00
Carbine 400–800.00

Whitney-Remington rolling block:

Sporting rifle 250–750.00
Lightweight sporting rifle 500–1,000.00
Carbine 400–800.00
Shotgun 150–350.00

Whitney-Burgess-Morse lever-action:

Sporting rifle 500–1,250.00
Military rifle 1,000–2,500.00
Carbine 1,000–2,750.00

Whitney-Kennedy lever-action repeater:

Sporting rifle 300–1,200.00
Military rifle 1,000–2,500.00
Carbine 1,000–2,500.00

Whitney-Scharf lever-action repeater:

Sporting rifle 500–1,250.00

Military rifle 1,500–4,500.00
Carbine 1,500–3,500.00

Double-barrel shotgun 250–500.00

WINCHESTER FIREARMS

Model 1866 rifle:

First model rifle 7,500–20,000.00
As above: Carbine 2,500–10,000.00
Second model rifle 1,500–5,000.00
As above: Carbine 1,250–3,500.00
Third model rifle 1,250–5,000.00
As above: Carbine 1,000–3,500.00
As above: Musket 1,000–3,000.00

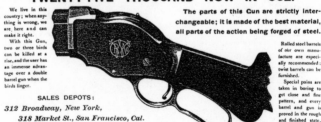

Fourth model rifle 1,250–5,000.00
As above: Carbine 1,000–3,500.00
As above: Musket 1,000–3,500.00

Model 1873:

Rifle 500–3,500.00
Carbine 750–3,500.00
Musket 750–3,500.00
.22 rimfire rifle 750–1,500.00

ONE IN A MILLION?

Model 1873 and 1876 "1 of 100" and "1 of 1000" rifles are among the rarest of firearms and are subject to fakery. If you are in the market for one of these rarities, bring the bank; they sell, when and if they come on the market, for many thousands of dollars and one recently topped all records for American firearms at just over $500,000.

Model 1876:

Rifle 650–2,500.00
Carbine 800–3,500.00
Musket 2,500–5,000.00

Model 1886:

Rifle 750–2,000.00
Lightweight rifle 500–1,000.00
Take-down rifle 600–1,200.00
Carbine 1,750–5,000.00

As above: Full stock 2,500–7,000.00
Musket 3,000–8,500.00

Model 71 rifle 500–1,500.00
Model 1892 rifle:

Rifle 350–750.00
Take-down model 500–1,000.00
Carbine 500–2,000.00
Musket 3,500–7,500.00

Model 53 rifle 500–1,000.00
Model 65 rifle 500–1,000.00
Model 1894 carbine 250–2,500.00
Model 1895 rifle:

Rifle 350–750.00
Take-down model 500–1,250.00
Carbine 500–3,500.00
Flat-side musket 4,000–10,000.00
Standard musket(s) 500–2,000.00

Single-shot rifle:

Three models, various calibers, barrel
lengths, and weights 250–10,000.00
High-wall/thick-wall express 1,000–2,500.00
Take-down .22 high-wall 450–900.00
High wall .22 musket 250–450.00

Winchester-Hotchkiss bolt-action:

Sporting rifle 350–750.00
Carbine 400–800.00

Musket 400–800.00
Army and Navy models 500–1,500.00

Winchester-Lee rifle 500–1,000.00
Model 1890 slide-action rifle:

First model 1,000–3,000.00
Second and third models 250–750.00

Double-barrel shotgun 1,000–3,500.00
Model 1887 lever-action shotgun 400–1,000.00
Model 1901 lever-action shotgun 400–1,000.00
Model 1893 slide-action shotgun 250–750.00
Model 1897 slide-action shotgun:

Standard grade 200–400.00
Trap gun 350–750.00
Pigeon gun 450–900.00
Riot gun 250–500.00
Trench gun 300–600.00

Additional Winchester firearms are listed in my first *Price Guide.*

LIMITED COVERAGE

There is more — much more. Antique American firearms date to the 1600s, continue through the romance of the famed "Kentucky" rifles, and end with all manner of collectible hammer and hammerless models. What follows is incomplete, only a synopsis of this history, and those who want to know more are urged to read and study other books on this subject beginning with Norm Flayderman's wonderful Guide to Antique American Firearms, *which is must reading for anyone with an interest in these things.*

KENTUCKY RIFLES

Transition-era rifles	500–25,000.00+
1780-1830 models	500–10,000.00+
Heavy "Match" rifles	250–2,500.00
As above: converted to percussion	250–10.000.00

PERCUSSION RIFLES

Half-stock models	250–7,500.00
Plains rifles	250–7,500.00+
Bench-rest models	750–5,000.00
Schuetzen rifles	750–3,500.00
Breechloading percussion rifles	500–1,500.00

LEVER AND SLIDE ACTIONS

Bullard sporting rifle	500–5,000.00
Burgess rifles and shotguns	350–2,000.00
Evans lever-action rifles	500–1,500.00
Henry lever-action rifles	3,500–25,000.00+
Jennings rifles	500–2,500.00
Smith-Jennings rifles	2,500–5,000.00
Robinson rifles	750–1,250.00
Savage lever-action rifles	500–3,500.00
Volcanic rifles	1,000–10,000.00+

SINGLE-SHOT RIFLES

Buck rifle	250–750.00
Bullard rifles	500–3,500.00
Farrow Arms	1,500–5,000.00

Holden rifles	500–2,500.00
Hopkins & Allen	250–1,500.00
Howard rifles	250–500.00
Lee rifle	250–500.00
Maynard patent rifles	500–3,500.00
Peabody/Peabody-Martini	1,250–5,000.00
Wurfflein tip-up rifles	250–2,500.00

REVOLVING RIFLES

These rarities are best left to the museums and the dean of antique firearms—Norm Flayderman. Again—you cannot even think about collecting firearms before you read Flayderman's Guide to Antique American Firearms. *Get a copy today.*

SHOTGUNS

Single-barrel flintlocks	500–1,000.00+
Double-barrel flintlocks	1,000–2,500.00+
As above: converted to percussion	250–750.00+
Single-barrel percussion shotguns	200–750.00
Double-barrel percussion shotguns	250–750.00

DAMASCUS SHOTGUNS

The following shotguns are all "Damascus barrel" shotguns and— as such—are dangerous. These "twist steel" barrels will not withstand today's high-power shotshells. I have listed only those shotguns of particular collector interest and many company names, from American Arms to the Wilkes-Barre Gun Company, have been left out. These unnamed "twist steel" shotguns are generally valued from $100 to $1,000 depending on grade and condition.

DAMASCUS BARREL SHOTGUNS

Baker Gun Company 100–500.00
As above: Three-barrel drilling 300–750.00
Charles Daly: imported 250–750.00
Fox Gun Company 100–350.00
Hollenbeck Gun Company: Three barrel gun
valves 350–1,000.00
Lefever Arms 200–500.00
Parker Brothers:

       Early models 350–1,250.00
       Others 350–10,000.00

L. C. Smith 350–1,500.00
Spencer Arms 200–400.00
Young Repeating Arms 400–800.00

Sporting Knives

When I was in grade school back in the 1930s a boy was undressed if he didn't have a knife. We all wore high-cut lace boots and the bootmakers put a pocket on the right side of the right boot to hold a jackknife. Going to school without that pocket filled and ready for mumbleypeg was worse than being caught in a pair of short pants. A knife was a knife to me in those long-ago school days just so long as it cut the circle and captured territory, and it wasn't until one of our group stuck his knife right through another boy's foot and my father had to come to school to retrieve his favorite whittling knife from the princial's extensive collection that I began to learn about knives and their use and value.

Knives and I have come a long way from those days of the Depression and New Deals and I like to think that some of the things I have learned will keep you out of the proverbial woodshed, where I learned my first lesson more than fifty years ago. As prices of both new and good pre-owned knives soar, even the sharpest buyers take a licking now and then and knowledge must be continually honed if one is to avoid the alternative use for a strop. If a beginning collector hopes to avoid such punishment, he or she should learn all they can about this complex subject. And there is no better place to start than the early 1800s, when the needs of a new nation reshaped the knife forever.

Collectible knives come in all shapes and sizes and—it goes without saying—all price ranges. The knives we are concerned with here serve sporting purposes and, unless you consider duels and knife fights to be 'sports,' the so-called "Bowie knife" has no place on these pages. But I ask you, if you were sitting where I am, could you leave Rezin P. Bowie and his little brother James out of any treatise about American knives? I thought not. Not only are "Bowie knives" the beginning and the end for many dedicated collectors, but the foundation upon which all modern sheath knives are based. It is with this latter thought in mind that I continue.

Historians disagree on the origin of the earliest Bowie knives that were handcrafted for Rezin Bowie, but it is fairly well accepted that the first of these blades was the work of blacksmith Jesse Smith and finished by Rezin himself. Later makers included Henry Schively of Philadelphia, Rees Fitzpatrick, and James Black — and there are those who insist that each of these men, together with others whose names are lost to history, fabricated the knife that saved Colonel James Bowie's life in an 1827 fight with Major Norris Wright. Be that as it may, history tells us it was Schively who introduced the eight-inch blade, sharpened false edge, and slant clip, thereby becoming the 'father' of the classic clip-point "Bowie knives" that followed. I could ramble on and on about classic and collectible "Bowies" but I have made my point — Rezin Bowie and his little brother started something that knows no end. Those of you who wish to pursue "Bowie knives" and their history will find Robert Abels's two books, *Bowie Knives* and *Classic Bowie Knives*, of great interest and well worth the time and expense of finding them on the used and rare book market. Any serious collector of Bowie knives should also consider David Hewett's enlightening and entertaining article about the "original" knife in the July, 1990, issue of *Maine Antiques Digest*.

Considering the size and shape of things, it is a far step from a large sheath knife to a small folding pocketknife, but each arrived in our country with a long European lineage. Sheath knives are adaptations of the Spanish dagger, Scottish dirk, and other Old-Country designs. The common pocketknife has changed little since the 17th century. Folding knives can be traced to the first-century Romans and are documented in literature dating to 1672, and there is little doubt the "spring-blades" of Sheffield, England, were brought to North American shores with the settlers of Roanoke, Jamestown, and Plymouth colonies.

American knife manufacturing was unknown until 1832 when the cutler Henry Schively introduced Rezin Bowie's design to a ready market and the enterprising John Russell founded his Green River Works in Greenfield, Massachusetts — the very first American cutlery company. Russell's "Green River" sheath knives joined the Bowie blades of numerous makers and together they played as important a part in winning the American West as did the Colt and Winchester firearms. If we carry this early knife history just a bit farther we discover that John Russell's early models #1000, 1100, and 1200 were in fact Bowie-style knives available with five-, six-, seven-, eight-, and nine-inch blades.

If all this seems confusing, it is. But there is a world of difference between early, handmade Bowie knives and those manufactured by Russell, Sheffield, and others. The difference is that the manufactured variety are collectible and valuable, while the early antique Bowie knives are worth their weight in gold. But enough of Rezin and James Bowie; my publisher begrudges wasted space and we need to move on to pocketknives before he puts his foot down.

John Russell and other early American cutlers such as the Meriden Cutlery Company, the Waterville Company, and Lamson and Goodnow produced thousands upon thousands of mediocre knives in the 1840s and 50s. It was not until James Roberts founded the New York Knife Company in Walden, New York, that the American pocketknife equaled the quality of the imported blades from Sheffield, England. Estimates of the number of American cutlery companies operating in the days after the Civil War vary from 600 to several thousand, but blades that collectors seek are, with rare exceptions, of later manufacture and beginning collectors are warned that age alone is not a prerequisite for value.

Early knives of great value include the Russell "Barlow" with one or two blades, which was made from the 1870s; W. L. Marble's

"Safety Hunting Knife," dating from 1902; many offerings by the Union Cutlery Company, whose later blades carried the "Ka-Bar" markings; and, of course, the ever popular "Keen Kutter" knives made by the Walden Knife Company. It would be impossible to conclude this all-too-short listing without naming two of America's most popular and widely collected knives—those manufactured by Remington and Winchester. Remington made and sold fine knives from 1920 until 1940 and the eve of World War II. Winchester entered the knife business when it merged with the E. C. Simmons Company in 1923 and moved the Simmons'-owned Walden Knife Company to New Haven to manufacture—you guessed it—Winchester knives. The company made quality knives until 1933.

It was difficult to compile the list of collectible sporting knife prices that we will get to in a minute. Difficult not because there is a lack of material on the market, but because there are so many non-sporting knives that are truly collectible from a knife nut's point of view that it becomes necessary to draw a line between sporting and non-sporting blades. Sporting knives come in all shapes, sizes, and price ranges. There are skinning knives, fishing knives, bird hunting knives, and stainless steel knives for saltwater sportsmen that come with and without marlin spikes in both sheath and folding models. Non-sporting knives include many models of both sheath and folding designs that serve no sporting purpose. I have not included daggers, boot knives, "Rambo-style" monstrosities, or any of the truly wonderful specimens inlaid with gold or sheathed in old ivory (sporting or not, only a fool would take a knife of that caliber out in the weather or expose it to the harsh treatment sportsmen give their tools). I trust my thin line is drawn where it will do you the most good in evaluating this or that knife.

Before perusing the following prices and buying or selling a particular knife you should know that—unless stated to the contrary—the prices listed are for knives in mint or near-mint condition. Flaws of any kind reduce the values greatly and heavily used or abused examples are next to worthless unless they are very, very rare.

Sellers should realize they can expect no more than half the listed price and buyers should remember that the time-worn phrase *caveat emptor* is still sharp advice. I have kicked around the sporting collectibles scene for more years than I care to remember and the sharpest dealers I encounter are those who prune the public with worthless cutlery. Know who you are dealing with and be sure they stand behind what they sell. You can put a Band-aid on a cut but your wallet and ego are not so easily repaired.

The following knives are listed alphabetically by maker. To avoid confusion, sheath knives and pocket or folding knives are listed separately. Sheaths are included unless stated otherwise. All prices are from 1991 and 1992.

BUCK KNIVES

Sheath Knives:

Model 116, 3 1/2" blade. Satin finish, as new 25.00
3 1/4" blade skinner, satin finish 40.00
Model 119ST, 6" Bowie blade, satin finish 110.00
Model 123 Lakemate, 6 1/2" filet blade. As new . . . 20.00
Model 125 Streamate, 4 1/2" filet blade. As new . . 20.00

Pocketknives:

Model 317, 5 1/4" closed, 2-blade jacknife. Light
use 110.00
Creek 4 1/4" closed, 3-blade stockman. As new . . . 45.00
XLTI Titanium Model 560, 5 closed lockback.
New with sheath 50.00
Model 531, 4 3/4" closed 2-blade trapper. As new
with sheath 125.00
Model 513, 3 3/8" closed lockback. As new 40.00
Model 515, 2 7/8" closed lockback. As new 35.00
Model 110, Custom 5" closed lockback. Mint 135.00

PASSING THE BUCK

Twenty-five years ago a brash but knowledgeable knife writer stated: "Buck knives are the most overrated knives in America today." Buck has enjoyed great success in the quarter century since then, but today's collectors shun these blades and many sportsmen find them fragile. If you want a knife that will be worth at least what you paid for it at some point down the road, perhaps you too should pass the Buck.

CAMILLUS KNIVES

Pocketknives:

      3 1/4" closed lockback, wood scales, used 25.00

      USA 4 1/2" closed stainless sailor's knife. As new . 30.00

      3 5/8" closed Cub Scout knife. Used 25.00

      4 1/2" closed two-blade trapper. As new in box . . . 35.00

      A.G. Russell CM-2 5" closed granddaddy barlow.

      As new 40.00

CONTRACT CAMILLUS KNIVES

In addition to making knives with their own brand names, Camillus has always been a contract cutlery company, providing Sears, Woolworths, and, more recently, Buck and A. G. Russell with knives. I am prejudiced, but the Camillus brand that warms my heart is their own Mumbleypeg.

CASE KNIVES

Sheath Knives:

      Model 147 3 3/4" blade, walnut handle. As new . . . 75.00

Model 161 4 1/2" blade, stag grip. As new 125.00
Model E-23 5" blade with mottled pearl grips.
As new 175.00
Model 208 as above with black rubber grips.
As new 100.00
261-KNIFAX combination 5" knife/4 1/2" axe.
Walnut grip 350.00
Model 3-FINN 4 1/4" blade, leather handle. As new   40.00
Model M3-FINN as above with 3" blade 35.00
Model 317 5" blade with leather/fiber handle.
As new 100.00
Model 392 4 1/2" blade with ivory handle. As new   150.00
Model 561-deluxe 5" knife/4 1/2" axe. Stag handle. Rare
400.00
Model 661-KNIFAX as above. Rare 500.00
Model 961-deluxe 5" blade. Imitation pearl handle.
As new 400.00
Model Midget 2 1/4" blade. Pearl handle. Mint . . . 175.00
Model Machete made in 1942. As new 125.00

Pocketknives:
Model 61213 5 1/2" swell center blade,
green bone handle 500.00
Display knife (pre-1940) 12" blade. As new 1,200.00
Model Zipper 5 1/2" switchblade, green bone
handle. Mint 4,000.00
As above with stag handle 3,000.00
M100 3 1/4" press button slide blade. As new,
various handles 100.00
Model 11031SH 3 1/16" jack, walnut handles.
As new 125.00
Model 6143 5" Daddy Barlow. Various
liners/handles, up to 175.00
Model 61048 Sportsman's Jack, green bone handle   150.00
As above with bone or red bone handles 50.00

Model 3165 5 1/2" folding hunter, yellow
composition handle 400.00
Model 5165 as above with stag handles 400.00
Model 6165 as above with green bone handles . . .   450.00
Model 5171L as above, switchblade,
stag handles 1,200.00
Other folding hunter models priced from
35.00 to 1,200.00

THE CASE FOR CASE

There are probably more collectors of Case knives than of any other brand of knife and Case collectors can probably tell more from a Case knife's markings than you or I could ever hope to know. Code letters and numbers are a part of the Case mystique and are something you must learn before you whet your appetite for these collectible blades. The sheath and jackknives listed here are only the tip of a large iceberg. To see it all you must do your homework and the material listed at the end of this chapter should prove helpful. A word of advice—Case came under new management in 1972 and again in 1989 and the jury is still out on the products of these later organizations, but good examples of Case knives made before 1972 are like money in the bank.

CATTARAUGUS KNIVES

Pocketknives:

Model 11709 4" blade Small Hunter,
stag handles 75.00
Model 12099 4 1/2" Deer Slayer with stag handles.
As new 150.00
Model 12819 5 3/8" King of the Woods with stag
handles. Mint 500.00

Model 21419 come-apart camp knife. 3 3/4", stag
handle. Mint 125.00
Folding machete, 11 1/4" blade. Used and dull 75.00

DOZIER, BOB

Sheath Knives:
  3 1/2" blade skinner. Stag handle. As new 465.00
  3 5/8" blade Drop point, stag. As new 485.00
  As above with micarta handle 345.00
  3" drop point blade. Mastadon bone handle.
  As new 445.00
  As above with surface ivory handle 745.00

Two New "Bare Bones" Knives:
  DK-2CM 3 1/4" drop point, micarta scales, Kydex
  sheath. 115.00
  DK-3CM as above sans finger groove 115.00

HANDMADE BLADES

Bob Dozier's name is the first of the fine cutlers listed here. He and his contemporaries are worthy of your serious consideration, not only as makers of fine knives, but for investments as well. A fine, well-made knife is a pleasure to own and use and a good hedge against inflation.

GERBER KNIVES

Pocketknives:
  3 5/8" closed midlock blade. Wood scales 30.00

4 1/2" lockback. Brass frame with wood inlay.
Light wear 35.00

Sheath Knives:

Blackie Collins model. 3 3/8" sawtooth blade. Used   65.00
R.W. Loveless design boot knife. As new 150.00
6 3/4" blade Guardian II. Mint 85.00
Model C-475 4 5/8" blade hunter 75.00
Model C-425 4 1/4" blade hunter 75.00
Model 473 5" blade boot knife. Mint 75.00

HALE, LLOYD

Pocketknives:

Lloyd Hale's folding knives are wonderful. They are also too expensive to go awandering and therefore not included here.

Sheath Knives:

4 1/8" boot knife. Micarta handle. Mirror finish . .   475.00
5 3/4" blade hunter. Compass is stag handle.
No sheath 395.00
12 1/4" blade Bowie. Nickel silver hilt. Stag handle.
No sheath 650.00
4" drop-point blade hunter. Stag handle.
Mirror finish 525.00

KA-BAR KNIVES (UNION CUTLERY COMPANY)

Pocketknives:

Dog's Head Models:

22 Bullet model 4 1/2" blade with stag handle . . .   500.00
62 Bullet model as above with bone handle 450.00
Model 6191LG 5 1/4" blade with bone handle . . .   450.00

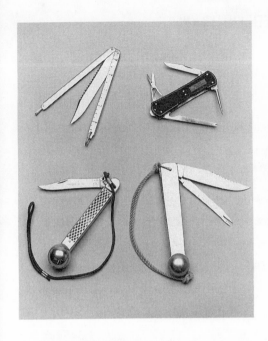

SPECIAL PURPOSE KNIVES include these collectible examples by Ka-Bar (*top left and right*) and the Puma (*bottom left*), and Italian "Priest" models. Photograph by David Allen for Bob Lang.

Other old Dog's Head models with various handle materials. To 400.00
New Dog's Head knives 50.00

THE "K" KNIVES

The "K" knives — those by KA-BAR of Union Cutlery manufacture and KEEN KUTTER from the Simmons'-controlled Walden Knife Company — are eagerly sought by collectors. The best of the KA-BAR knives are stamped "KA-BAR–Olean, New York," the large folding hunter models, and those with genuine stag handles. All KEEN KUTTER knives are collected and, again, those with large blades and stag grips top the list. After 1923, KEEN CUTTER was dropped in the new Simmons Hardware/Winchester merger and the blades were immediately marked "Winchester," which we will get to shortly. Look sharp and learn about your subject before you buy.

KEEN KUTTER KNIVES

Pocketknives:

Model K0147 3/4" Muskrat, two narrow 4" blades   185.00
Model K0247, two 3 7/8" blades (spear and clip).
As new 100.00
Model K170 4 1/4" (Barlow) single 3 3/4" blade.
As new 45.00
Model K01881 (Barlow) 3 1/2" spey and pen blades.
Stag handle 100.00
Model K01884 as above with 3 1/8" blades 100.00
Model K02070 as above with 3" blades 50.00

LOVELESS, ROBERT

Sheath Knives:

3 3/4" (Lawndale) skinner. Micarta handle.
Used, fine 1,545.00
5 1/2" (Safariland) hunter with finger-grooved stag,
used 1,695.00
As above with cocobolo handle, used 1,695.00
3 3/4" (Riverside) drop-point blade. Stag handle.
Mint 2,495.00

A LEGEND

It all began in 1953 when the always irascible Bob Loveless went to Abercrombie & Fitch in New York to buy a Bo Randall knife and was informed that there was a long waiting list. Typically, he said: "Hell, I'll make my own," and did just that. A few years later his "Jersey Belle" knives were the A & F house knife and setting sales records, to boot. By the mid-1970s Loveless had refined his style and was considered by many the most gifted cutler in the world. Loveless is indeed a legend.

MARBLES KNIVES

Pocketknives:

Folding hunter with hard rubber handle 700.00
As above with stag handle 600.00

Sheath Knives:

Woodcraft 3 3/8" blade, leather handle and
aluminum butt. Good 115.00
As above in mint condition 175.00
As above with stag handle in poor condition 95.00
As above in mint condition 285.00
Ideal 5" blade hunting knife with leather handle.
Fine 145.00
Ideal 6" blade hunting knife with stag handle.
Very good 200.00
Expert 5" blade hunting knife (without blood groove).
Good 125.00
As above with stag handle 195.00

MORSETH KNIVES:

Model 3 Alaskan Hunter 4 3/4" blade, stag handle.
Mint 230.00
Model 4 Cascade Skinner 4 1/8" blade, stag
handle. As new 230.00
Model 5 Wilderness Knife 6" blade, stag handle.
Mint 220.00
Model 8 boot knife 4 1/4" blade, ivory micarta
handle. Mint 295.00
Michigan Sportsman 4" clip-point blade, micarta
handle. Used 150.00

PAL CUTLERY COMPANY

Sheath Knives:

Model RH35 USN Mark I 5 1/4" fighting knife.
Used 60.00
Another, as above. Fine 100.00
WW II 4 7/8" blade fighting knife. Fine 125.00

Note: These designs and many others originated with Remington. In
       1940 PAL bought the Remington stock and designs. They made
       knives until 1953.

PUMA KNIVES

Folding fisherman's knife with scale and priest.
Fine 150.00
As above, new in box 70.00

YOU GET WHAT YOU PAY FOR

*The old adage that you get what you pay for is a truth that cannot
be ignored, but it is equally true that you pay for what you get.
Prices in this book are taken from actual sales and/or dealer
prices; they do not come off the top of my head. The identical Puma
fisherman's knives listed illustrate a point. These knives were both
sold, the first at a fishing tackle auction and the second through a
knife list. As a result the preceding adages should probably be
amended to include: you pay for where you buy it.*

RANDALL, W.D. "Bo"

Sheath Knives:

Model 8 Trout & Bird knife with 4" blade. Used
and pitted 175.00
Model 1, 7" blade, micarta handle. Mint 295.00

AN ALL-TIME FAVORITE knife is this "Trout and Bird Knife" by Randall of Orlando, Florida, who provided the photograph for this book. In my youth this knife was a bargain at less than twenty dollars and is an even better buy today at about ten times that amount.

As above with stag handle 295.00

Model 1, 6" blade, micarta handle. Mint 295.00

As above with stag handle 295.00

Model 5 Camp & Trail with 5" blade and stag handle.
Mint 290.00

As above with 6" blade 290.00

Model 7 Fisherman-Hunter with 5" blade,
stag handle 285.00

Model 12 Sportsman's Bowie with 6" blade. Mint . 265.00

Note: Older Randall knives in fine condition are much more valuable than the newer ones listed here.

OUT OF THIS WORLD

It is a far step from a garage in Florida in 1936 to outer space in the 1970s, from a single knife based on an early Scagle blade to thousands of knives designed to the customer's satisfaction without losing the personal touch that made them what they are. A far step indeed, but the late Bo Randall took the handmade knife from the workshop to the people with both skill and dignity. He was both out of this world and down to earth, a knife maker for his time and for the ages.

REMINGTON KNIVES

Sheath Knives:

4 1/4" blade skinner. Leather handle, used 60.00

Another 55.00

Model RH251 4" blade hunter. Girl Scout etching,
worn, used 75.00

Model RH50 4 1/2" blade hunter/skinner.
Light pitting 60.00

6" blade hunter. Leather handle, very good
condition 95.00

Another as above 85.00

Pocketknives:

Model R6949 3" closed pen knife. Light putting and
use............................... 25.00

Boy Scout knife 3 5/8" blade (broken).
Used and pitted 75.00

As above with 3 3/4" blade. Used 100.00

3 3/4" closed knife with blade and screwdriver.
Wood handle. Used 250.00

Model R213 with bone handle. As new 200.00

Model R293 with brown bone handle. Mint 1,500.00

Model R1253 with brown bone handle. As new . 1,200.00

The following Remington pocketknives were made beginning in 1982 by Camillus and other manufacturers. The
"bullet" models have appreciated in value, but the
others ... *Caveat emptor*:

Model 1303 (1984) 4 1/2" closed lockback.
New in box 190.00

Model 1173L (1984) 3 5/8" closed lockback.
New in box 275.00
Another as above 200.00
Model R1173 (1983) 3 5/8" two-blade trapper.
New in box 275.00
Model R1615 (1988) 5" closed jackknife.
New in box 75.00

BITING THE BULLET

Remington "bullet" knives are eagerly sought after collectibles and, as such, expensive. These and other early Remington blades have mystic and confusing markings that you must learn before you get down to the business of buying and, believe me, it is a business. Fortunately the Remington catalogs from the 1920s and 30s have been reproduced and will teach you that "R" means pocketknife, numbers from R-1 through R-2999 are jackknives, and that the last digit indicates one of ten possible handle materials. I'll tell you that R-1 is a jackknife with redwood handles, but from here on you are on your own.

RUANA, R. H.

Sheath Knives:

4 3/8" skinner. Green stag handle with grooves.
Made by Rudy 300.00
5 1/8" hunter. Stag inlays, owner's monogram,
used 135.00
4 1/2" blade skinner. Stag inlays, scratched 135.00
5" blade skinner. Stag inlays. As new 275.00
6" blade hunter. Stag inlays. Used 175.00
As above, made by Rudy 285.00

A. G. RUSSELL

In April 1974 Knife Digest, *prior to publication of its first issue, named A. G. Andy Russell the first member of its Hall of Fame for his tireless work on behalf of others. Today, more than a quarter century later, Russell's good name continues. As a cutler, a seller, and promoter of others' work, he has few peers. Any interested collector should subscribe to "The Cutting Edge" catalogs of pre-owned knives. Send $15.00 to 1705 Highway 71 North, Springdale, Arkansas, 72764. Tell them I sent you.*

RUSSELL, A. G.

Pocketknives:

"Arkansas Toothpick" 3 1/2" blade. Ebony handle.
As new 60.00
As above, with stag handle 75.00
Another. Scratched 45.00
Sailor's knife. Combination blade and marlin spike.
As new 75.00

Sheath Knives:

Model LV-DS (Loveless style) 3 3/4" drop-point
hunter. Micarta 295.00
Model LV-DBR as above with India stag handle.
New 375.00
Model AGMK 9 1/2" blade Bowie with Zytel handle.
As new 100.00
Model AGMK-2S as above with stag handle 170.00
Model AGST "Sting" 3 1/4" double-edged blade.*
Rosewood handle 55.00

BANNED BLADES

Some states, several cities, and some towns have outlawed double-edged knives as well as switch-blades. Check your local laws, not after you purchase such a knife, but before. The money you save will be your own.

RUSSELL (Green River Works)

Sheath Knives:

Model 78 stag handle hunting knife with 6" blade.
Pitted 125.00
Model 1000 Bowie-style hunting knife, stag handle.
No sheath 175.00
Model 215 Cocobolo handle sheath knife. 4 1/2" blade.
Pitted 85.00

Pocketknives:

Model 42 Barlow. Two blades, white
bone handle . . . . scarce
Model 603 Barlow. Single blade (3 3/8"),
bone handle. Pitted 1,200.00

Note: Model 52 had buffalo-horn handles.

SCHATT & MORGAN KNIVES

Pocketknives:

Model 396 4" clip blade, imitation stag handle. As
new 150.00
Model 1166 3 5/8" blade, nickel silver bolsters.
Used 200.00

Model 37193. As above with 3 1/8" blade 200.00
Model 47283. As above with 3" blade. New 50.00

SCHRADE CUTLERY

Pocketknives:

Model 114 3/4" fisherman's knife with 5" blade.
Stag handle 300.00
Model 1083 sportsman's knife with 5" blade.
Stag handle. As new 150.00
Model 1147 3/4" Barlow with 5" clip blade. Pitted   125.00
Model 1514J dagger-style, clip-point, push-button.*
4" blade 150.00
Model G1543 3/4" folding clip-point, push-button.*
4 7/8" blade 400.00
Model 1543 3/4" hunting knife. As above,*
stag handle 300.00

SWITCHBLADES

Push-button, or "switchblade" knives, are illegal in most states and in 1957 interstate traffic in them was banned by the federal government.

WESTERN CUTLERY COMPANY

Sheath Knives:

Model L66 4 1/2" hunter with leather handle. As
new 20.00
4" clip blade Boy Scout knife with BSA emblem.
Used, no sheath 55.00
5 3/4" blade fighting knife. Leather handle. Fine . .   50.00

WINCHESTER KNIVES:

Model 1060 Texas Jack 4 1/8" blade. Celluloid
handle. Mint 225.00
Model 1611 jackknife with 3 1/4" blade. Scratched .   50.00
Model 1920 folding hunter with 5 1/4" blade.
Bone handle. As new 1,000.00
Model 1950 clip-point lockback. 6 3/4" blade.
Stag handle. As new 1,200.00
Model 2701 Barlow with 3 1/2" blade, bone handle.
Used 125.00
Another, as new 225.00
Model 3944 gunstock with 3 3/4" blade. Fine   . . .   250.00

The following knives were manufactured by Blue Grass Cut-
lery under license from the Olin Corporation beginning in
1987:

W-15 One Blade Toothpick. New 100.00
W-15 1927 Lockback folding hunter with 5 3/8"
blade. New 100.00
W-15 3904 Whittler (3 5/8"). New 100.00

The list goes on with lesser values. The most collectible
and therefore valuable Winchester knives were made from
1923 until the early 1930s.

SUGGESTED READING

If you are not a knife nut, and even if you are a beginning collector,
the listings in this volume may be adequate. If you are serious about
the subject you will know that they are not. No single chapter in any
single book can do justice to this complex and competitive subject. If
you have whet your appetite or cut your teeth here, that is a start.

Learn all you can before you buy. The following list is a step on the road to success.

A History of the John Russell Cutlery Co. –R. L. Merriman
Bowie Knives (Robert Abels) –W. G. Keener
Classic Bowie Knives –Robert Abels
The Case Knife Story –A. P. Swayne
American Knives –Harold Peterson
A History of Knives –Harold Peterson
The Cutting Edge –A. G. Russell (periodical)

Marbles, Remington, and Winchester catalog reprints, and more.

SPORTING ART

Sporting art takes many forms — photography, cartoons, fine bronzes, oil paintings, watercolors, etchings, carvings — and all of it is collected and therefore collectible and worthy of your serious consideration. In my first *Price Guide* I listed collectible prints by a great many artists and, if this is your particular area of interest, I respectfully refer you to that volume. In this edition I explore all manner of sporting art sold at wildfowl decoy and fishing tackle auctions in the past two years. I know this is not the art market that receives all the attention in the press, but it is our market — yours and mine — and deserves your attention. I hope you agree.

As you thumb through this section you will see figures in brackets after each offering like (000–0000); these are the seller's estimate of low and high selling price. Often, particularly in the market that exists as I write this in 1992, the owner has put a reserve (a price below which the collectible will not be sold) on his consignment. If this price is not bid, the item is not sold. I have included these estimates in this section simply to show you, the sporting art market, as some of the offerings listed here failed to sell and the estimated selling price is your only clue to presumed value.

The following list of sporting art is arranged in alphabetical order by artist. I am indebted to Gary Guyette, Bob Lang, Richard Oliver, and Frank Schmidt for their cooperation and illustrations.

ABBOTT, ROBERT

1981 Trout Unlimited print & stamp: Framed in
excellent condition. (175–225) 150.00

Theodore Gordon Flyfishers print: In excellent
condition. One of 300. (200–300) 140.00

BARKER, AL

Watercolor "Early Morning" : Matted and framed, in
excellent condition. (200–250) 50.00

Watercolor "Surf Fisherman": Matted and framed,
in excellent condition. (200–250) 125.00

BENSON, FRANK

Etching "Winter Waterfowling": Matted and
unframed, in good condition. (2,000–2,500) 1,800.00

Etching of Canada geese: Mislabled as pen and ink.
Matted and framed with some foxing. (300–500) . . .   450.00

BICKFORD (19TH CENTURY ARTIST) MILLS FALLS, NH

Pastel of hooked salmon: With minor damage.
Framed. (1,000–2,000) 500.00

Pastel of trout: Minor scratches and breakage to
frame, otherwise excellent. (750–1000) 500.00

Pastel of hooked trout: Framed and in excellent
condition. (750–1,000) 900.00

BISHOP, BAINBRIDGE

Oil painting of trout: Rod and reel by Orvis, in
excellent condition. (6,000–7,000) . . . .   NS

Oil painting of three trout hanging on branch: Needs
restoration. (600–800) 300.00

BISHOP, RICHARD

Oil painting of seven mallards set to land: In
exceptional condition. (12,000–15,000) . . . .   NS

*Oil painting of mallards decoying to set of Delaware
decoys*: (9,000–12,000) . . . .   NS

Four signed Christmas cards: (400–600) 200.00

As above 200.00

Dry point "Over the Sun": (300–350) 145.00

Another "Bog Sprites": (250–350) 275.00

Another "Mallards Pitching: (250–300) 300.00

Another "Blacks & Greenheads": (250–300) 170.00

Another "Timber Mallards": (350–550) 300.00

Another "Thru the Timber": (250–350) 200.00

Another "On the Stalks": (250–350) 190.00

Another "Jack Pat": (250–350) 160.00

UNLIMITED

*No one doubted Richard Bishop's talent when he was working on
the myriad forms he perfected in various mediums, nor are his
talents questioned today. Unfortunately, Bishop signed his etchings
and prints but refused to limit them, selling as many as he could.
This limits their value to collectors.*

BOYER, RALPH

Etching of an angler: In excellent condition with
soiled mat. (75–100) 355.00

CLARK, ROLAND

Pair of watercolors: Pintail and redheads: Each is
3" × 4" and excellent. (1,600–2,500) 2,800.00

Derrydale print "Sanctuary: G.W. Teal": Trimmed,
in fine condition. (550–650) 450.00

F. Lowe print "Journey's End": Fine condition.
(700–900) 650.00

Etching (duck stamp print): Without stamp, in very
good condition. (1,500–2,000) 300.00

Etching "Captain Billy's Rig": In excellent
condition (1,800–2,200) 1,175.00

Etching of scoters flying: With slight discoloration.
(200–400) 200.00

Etching "Dead Canvasback": With minor crimping
at the print's edges. (200–500) 225.00

DENTON FISH (CHROMOLITHOGRAPHS)

Set of four different trout: Double matted and
framed. (150–200) 225.00

Set of four warm-water fish: Framed as above.
(150–200) 200.00

Set of five including trout and salmon: Framed in
cherry. (225–300) 225.00

ETTINGER, CHURCHILL

*Limited edition print "Rainy Day–Restigouche
River"*: In fine condition. Framed. (350–450) 400.00

Etching "Black Ducks at Dusk": Signed and in very
good condition. (200–300) 75.00

Etching "Dropping Broadbill": In fine condition with
mat stains. (100–125) 100.00

Etching "Opening Day": Shows angler on rocky
shore. (200–300) 140.00

Etching "Strike": Shows two anglers in a canoe. In
excellent condition. (200–300) 210.00

Etching "Nearly Netted": Depicts angler netting his
fish. (150–225) 140.00

FOOTE, JIM

Oil on canvas of Nate Quinlin decoys: In very fine
condition. (2,000–3,000) 1,000.00

Oil on canvas of duck hunters on Lake Erie: In
excellent condition. (4,000–5,000) . . . .   NS

*Oil on canvas of two gunners in a sneak boat amid
decoys and ducks:* (5,000–7,000) . . . .   NS

FROST, A.B.

Two prints: "Good Luck" and "Bad Luck": From
Scribner's 1903 portfolio. Framed (900–1,100) 675.00

Two prints: "Ordered Off" and "Gun Shy": From
the 1903 portfolio. (800–1,200) 900.00

Hand-colored lithograph "Muskallonge Fishing": In
excellent condition. (50–75) 85.00

As above "Black Bass Fishing": (50–75) 65.00

As above with angler landing a trout: (50–75) 75.00

GRUPPE, EMILE

Oil painting of striped bass fishing at Bass Rocks: In
excellent condition. (8,000–10,000) . . . . NS

HAGERBAUMMER, DAVID

Watercolor of mallard pair in flight: Framed and in
good condition with some foxing. (250–400) 375.00

HUNT, LYNN BOGUE

Watercolor of rainbow trout: Signed and inscribed,
excellent. (1,750–2,000) 1,350.00

Five framed prints of anglers and leaping fish: (100–
150) 212.50

Print of "Ring-Necked Pheasant": Signed by the
artist and inscribed. (100–200) 100.00

KEMP, OLIVER

Four fishing prints: Two are stained, in old period
frames. (400–600) 650.00

Horton (Bristol) poster: With minor wear and soiling.
(200–300) 165.00

KILBOURNE, S.A.

Print of leaping, hooked trout: Framed and in
excellent condition. (175–250) 275.00

Print of landed trout: Framed and in excellent
condition. (175–250) 250.00

Print of landed striped bass: Framed and in very
good condition. (175–200) 225.00

COLOR LITHOGRAPH by S. A. Kilbourne of a leaping trout that should be familiar to veteran Orvis customers.

KNAPP, J. D.

Two prints: "Day Break" and "The Inlet": With only
the second one signed. Both are framed. (600–900) .   250.00

Note: The buyer got a bargain.

LOGE, DANIEL

Oil painting of three widgeons in flight: In excellent
condition. Framed. (900–1,200) 350.00

MC DANIEL, HENRY

Limited edition print: (#165/300) Titled
"Anticipation," in excellent condition. (400–600) . . .   300.00

Another: (#55/350) Titled "The Return," matted
and framed. (150–200) 175.00

THE 10 PERCENT SOLUTION

Unlike most trends in this country that start in California, the fairly recent and now commonplace 10 percent buyer's premium on virtually all auction purchases had its beginnings in jolly old England. The premium was designed to attract sellers and their collectibles to the auction salesroom by giving them a bigger portion of the ultimate sale price, but has—in this writer's opinion—lost all semblance of its original intent.

PLEISSNER, OGDEN

Watercolor of hen green-winged teal speeding downwind: Excellent. (2,000–3,000) . . . . NS

Etching titled "Salmon Guide": Framed and in excellent condition. (1,700–2,000) 1,000.00

ETCHING by the wonderful Ogden Pleissner entitled "Salmon Guide" and a rare offering.

Print "Woodcock Cover": Signed, framed and
matted. Excellent. (400–600) 160.00

Print "The Lye Brook Pool": In excellent frame and
condition. (450–550) 250.00

*Print "Along the Granite Cliff — Moise River,
Quebec"*: Excellent. (400–500) 175.00

*Print commemorating the 75th anniversary of the
Angler's Club*: Excellent. (300–500) 400.00

POPE, ALEXANDER

Chromolithograph of redhead ducks (pair): In period
frame. Very good. (200–400) 200.00

Another-Buffleheads: (200–400) 275.00

REECE, MAYNARD

*Posters entitled "Trout" and "Salmon" depicting
these species*: Framed. (125–175) 175.00

RHEAD, LOUIS

Watercolor self-portrait of Rhead landing a trout:
Signed and inscribed. (4,000–6,000) 5,500.00

Watercolor: "A Strike": Signed and identified on
reverse. (2,500–3,500) 2,400.00

RIPLEY, A.L.

Duck stamp print: Framed with forty-two stamps in
individual mattings (1,800–2,400) 2,150.00

*Two etchings: "Flushed Grouse" and "Rising
Woodcock"*: Framed and excellent. (350–450) 150.00

SELF-PORTRAIT by Louis Rhead in watercolor. A unique piece of art by a famous fisherman/artist/writer.

Etching "Point on Quail": After an oil of the same
scene. Excellent. (250–350) 400.00

Print titled "A Turkey Drive": By Frost and Reed.
Signed and framed (400–600) 100.00

SCHALDACH, WILLIAM J.

Watercolor of leaping trout: In fine original frame.
(3,000–4,000) . . . .   NS

Watercolor of trout after fly: In fine matting and
frame. (2,500–3,500) . . . .   NS

Watercolor of sunfish and dangling worm: In
excellent condition. (2,400–2,800) . . . .   NS

Note: This sunfish watercolor sold in Vermont in 1991 for less than
$1,000.00.

TAYLOR, ARTHUR

Watercolor titled "Sunrise at Mercury Island": In
mint frame and condition. (1,400–1,600) 800.00

*Watercolor titled "Middle River" (*Cape Breton*)*: In
mint frame and condition. (750–1,000) 300.00

WARD, LEM

Oil painting of egret: Several dents in frame.
(300–500) . . . .   NS

Decoy template of merganser head: With authenticity
on back. (100–175) 225.00

WEILER, MILTON

Watercolor of hunters and ruffed grouse: In frame
with scratches. Excellent. (3,500–5.500) 3,000.00

Classic decoy series print: "Canada Goose": In fine
frame and condition. (50–100) 25.00

Another "Red-Breasted Merganser": (50–100) 20.00

Another "Black Duck": (50–100) 90.00

ZERN, ED

Cartoon of frog holding sign: Framed in black with
some minor flaws. (175–250) 175.00

Christmas cartoon greeting to the Truebloods:
Framed with tape marks. (175–200) 200.00

SELLING YOUR ART AT AUCTION

Should you decide that you have art to sell and want to go the "auction route" to dispose of it, remember that auction galleries take a percentage of the selling price. This varies from gallery to gallery, but generally runs from 10 to 20 percent, with more charged for lesser consignments.

ADVERTISING PINS AND SUCH

Not too many years ago I wore enough pins on my hat to give a strong man a bad back. But, with age, I have decided to let others talk through their hats and restrict my statements to the spoken and written varieties. With this in mind, I offer you this introduction to the amazing world of sporting pins, pin backs, and watch fobs. Make no mistake about it, this is only an introduction and in some future volume we will explore the oodles of "DU" pins, hunting and fishing badges, and other collectible pins and badges. Here we concern ourselves only with advertising material, and, believe me, that is enough for now.

WATCH FOBS, SPORTING ADVERTISING / PIN BACKS, & STICK PINS

The following watch fobs, pins, and stick pins are listed alphabetically by company or organization. Size is given in brackets as (0.000) and prices are those realized at auction by mail bidders. I am indebted to Bob and Beverly Strauss of Circus Promotions for the information.

AUSTIN POWDER COMPANY

Watch fob: Silver-plated, shows round powder can.
Good condition 150.00

Pin back: (.889) Multicolored, three dogs, rare.
Mint condition 150.00

BAKER GUNS

Shorebird whistle: (1.265) Promotion by jobber
selling these firearms in Boston. Rare 293.00

BALLSITE

Pin back: (.889) Red, white, and blue target design
in mint condition 41.00

Pin back: (.889) As above. Ballsite across center.
Mint 36.00

Pin back: (.889) As above. Ballsite and Empire in
triangle. Mint . . . .   NS

   Note: This pin back did not sell

BUFFALO ARMS

Pin: (Shield) Red, white, blue, and gold with "Get
It Done" in raised letters 20.00

COLT

Pin back: (.889) Only known example, shows the
familiar rear colt. Mint condition 385.00

DAISY

Pin back: (.889) Shows boy holding early air rifle.
Full color and mint condition 210.00

Pin back: (1.250) Red, blue, and yellow "Daisy
Cadet" in mint condition 54.00

As above: "Captain" added 138.00

DAVIS GUNS

Pin back: (.810) Gold with porcelain inserts in red
and blue. Excellent 30.00

DEAD SHOT

Stick pin: The famous falling mallard in gold.
Excellent condition 193.00

DOMINION

Stick pin: Gold pin with red "D" and blue shotshell .   149.00

Watch fob: (1.300) As above 475.00

DUPONT

Stick pin: Silver pin with quail. Rare . . . .   NS

Stick pin: Dog with DuPont ribbon 133.00

Stick pin: Bronze quail on oval 140.00

Pin back: (.889) The hard-to-find woodcock pin in
multicolor. Mint 317.00

Pin back: (.889) The so-called right-facing quail.
Mint 121.00

Pin back: (1.000) Full color pin with red DuPont
and two dogs 26.00

Pin back: Gold with hanging watch with a white
face 51.00

As above: With black watch face 100.00

Pin back: (1.250) Quail in multicolor in mint
condition 45.00

Another as above 28.00

As above: (.889) 64.00

THREE STICK PINS (*left to right*) DuPont, Winchester, and Hopkins & Allen together with ten assorted pin backs. Courtesy of Bob & Beverly Strauss.

DON'T GET STUCK

Like virtually all easily constructed sporting collectibles, advertising material of all kinds has been reproduced. Unfortunately this is true of all material listed here and it is necessary to remember the oft-repeated "Caveat Emptor." A small pin may give you only a small prick, but at these prices the sting can last a long time.

EC SMOKELESS POWDER

Pin back: (.889) Red on white "EC 1896" in mint condition 114.00

Pin back: (.889) Red, white, blue, and gold "EC and Schultze" 79.00

Tie tack: (.619) Black on orange "Shoot EC Powder" 51.00

HERCULES POWDER

Pin back: (.989) Red, white, and blue "Keep 'em
Shooting" in mint condition 61.00

Pin back: (.619) Black and orange 50.00

HOPKINS AND ALLEN

Stick pin: Gold revolver with name and address on
reverse. Mint 55.00

HUNTER ARMS

Pin back: (.892) Pink and white "The Hunter" 290.00

Pin back: (.892) "Ride A Hunter — Shoot A Smith"
in black and white 75.00

Pin back: (.889) "The Hunter" bicycles in black and
white. Mint 60.00

INFALLIBLE

Pin back: (.619) Blue and white "Shoot Infallible
Smokeless" 63.00

Tie tack: Exactly as above except for use 40.00

IVER JOHNSON

Pin back: (.889) White, blue, and gold bicycle
advertisement 15.00

Pin back: (.889) Bicycle ad with lady 31.00

LAFLIN AND RAND

Pin back: (1.250) Blue and gold "Smokeless" on
flag in mint condition 176.00

As above: "Infallible" on flag 36.00

As above: "Shotgun" on flag 35.00

As above: (1.000) 31.00

LOVELL

Pin back: (.889) "Lovell Diamond" on white pin 25.00

MULLERITE (N.Y. SPORTING GDS. CO.)

Oval pin back: "Mullerite" on pinkish pin back.
Mint 60.00

ORIENTAL POWDER MILLS

Pin back: (1.260) Gray can on white pin with
"Oriental Smokeless" on can. Rare 293.00

PETERS

Pin back: (.889) "Peters Ideal" in gold on reddish
background. Very rare 603.00

Pin back: (.889) Dog with quail coming through "P"
with red on white. Rare 560.00

Pin back: (.889) Mallard flying through "P" 109.00

As above: No lettering 78.00

As above: "Peters" on "P" 47.00

Pin back: (.889) "Peters New Victor" on light
green background. Very rare 660.00

Pin back: (.889) "Shoot Peters *Referee* Shells" with
shell in purple. Mint 90.00

Pin back: (.889) "Shoot Peters Shells" with red
high-brass shell on white 18.00

Pin back: (.889) "Steel Where Steel Belongs"
around red "P" 43.00

Stick pin: Gold with red "P" 63.00

As above: Black "P" 40.00

REMINGTON

Pin black: Oval multicolor "Remington Pump" 101.00

As above: "Remington Autoloading" 152.00

Pin back: (1.250) Multicolor quail on black 25.00

Pin back: (.889) Bears at work with "Steel Lined
Shells" in red, white, and blue 75.00

As above: With ".22 Repeater" 57.00

As above: With "Lesmok Cartridges" 55.00

Note: See also UMC/Remington listing

SCHULTZE POWDER

Pin back: (1.250) "For Shotguns I Always Use New
Schultze Powder," Annie Oakley with picture 420.00

SMITH GUNS

Stick pin: Multicolor oval showing the familiar
spaniel. Mint 110.00

SPORTING LIFE (MAGAZINE)

Pin oack: (1.000) Multicolor of man shooting with
red "Sporting Life —" on white background 42.00

STEVENS

Pin back: (.889) "Stevens Rifles —" in blue on
white. Mint 158.00

Pint back: (.889) "Stevens Shotguns — " in black on
tan. Mint 182.00

UMC

Pin back: (.889) Multicolor pin with Annie Oakley
under horseshoe and clover. Rare 463.00

Pin back: (.889) "Annie Oakley Shoots UMC
Ammunition" in black with red on white 348.00

Pin back: (.889) UMC and Annie Oakley in white
with red 800.00

UMC/REMINGTON

Pin back: Oval multicolor pin with UMC/
Remington pump. Mint 201.00

As above: Autoloading shotgun shown 235.00

Pin back: (.889) "Shoot UMC/Remington Arrow
and Nitro Club Shells" 72.00

As above: Remington and UMC reversed 50.00

WESTERN

Watch fob: Silver with porcelain insert of
"Western," in excellent condition 275.00

Stick pin: With "Western" in diamond 125.00

Pin back: (.889) "Shoot Western Field Shells" with
"Field" on red shell. Rare 357.00

As above: "Field" not on the shell 182.00

Pin back: (1.250) Multicolor red, white, and blue
with red diamond in blue. Rare . . . .   NS

TWO WATCH FOBS (*bottom left and center*) Dominion and Western; a rare shorebird whistle (*bottom right*) advertising Baker & Batavia guns; and twelve pin backs. Courtesy of Bob & Beverly Strauss.

Pin back: (1.250) Multicolor "Me For Springfield —
Oct 22–24" 432.00

Pin back: (.889) Orange and black with "White
Flyer" and company name and address 315.00

As above: With "Shooter's Favorite" 138.00

As above: With no lettering. Rare and cracked 140.00

Pin back: "Longest Run of 1907–274 Straight —"
in blue and red on white 176.00

WINCHESTER

Pin back: (1.250) Multicolor of Heil, Crosby, and
Gilbert (trapshooters). Mint condition 660.00

Pin back: (1.250) Multicolor of "The Wonderful
Tupperweins —" 501.00

Pin back: (1.250) Multicolor of Adolph Tupperwein who "Always shoots Winchester — ." Mint condition 303.00

Pin back: Oval multicolor shows J. R. Taylor 266.00

As above: Shows C. G. Spencer 185.00

As above: With variation 165.00

Stick pin "Ask for Winchester Nublack" on yellow shell 75.00

Stick pin: With "The 97.20% Shells" on yellow shell 145.00

CATALOGS

This is a short but important part of both this volume and the sporting collectibles market. Catalogs from the "Golden Age" are important to serious collectors for the detailed data they contain and to many of us who are often heard to say, "if only ..." as we thumb through these small treasures. For data and dreams, catalogs are hard to beat.

The following list is in alphabetical order and the prices are up-to-date.

ABBIE & IMBRIE

1889 wholesale catalog: 136 pages 450.00

1923 retail catalog: 174 pages 85.00

ABERCROMBIE, DAVID T.

1952 60th anniversary catalog: 167 pages 20.00

ABERCROMBIE & FITCH

Big Little Book of Fishing catalog: 1968 . . . . 10.00

Camping & Fishing catalog: 1956 . . . . 45.00

BATE, THOMAS H

Catalogue of Needles, Fish Hooks: 1860s 20.00

BRISTOL ROD COMPANY
Fishing Rods, Reels & Lines catalog #39 . . . . 130.00

J. T. BUEL
1913 catalog of spinners and baits: 30 pages 200.00

CHUBB, THOMAS H.
Chubb Rods Are Built on Honor: titled 1927 catalog . 425.00

DARBEE, E.B. & H.A.
Fly Patterns & Prices: 1952 . . . . 25.00

DICKERSON, LYLE
The Dickerson Rod catalog 110.00

HARDY BROTHERS
1919 Angler's Guide: 403 pages 95.00

1926 Angler's Guide: 372 pages 60.00

HAWES, H.W. & CO.
Rod catalog: 26 pages. Excellent 70.00

HEDDON
1939 "How To Catch More Fish" catalog 90.00

Another: 1942 . . . . 40.00

Fishing tackle catalog: 1952 . . . . 38.00

Another: 1953 . . . . 38.00

Another: 1962 . . . . 10.00

HEWITT, EDWARD

Hewitt Trout Fishing Specialties catalog: 1935 . . . . . . 65.00

ITHACA GUN COMPANY

Ithaca Guns: 1940 catalog with 26 pages 15.00

JOHNSON, H. J.

1885 price list of fishing tackle: With pictures 260.00

LEONARD ROD CO.

1974 catalog 40.00

Maxwell-era catalog 75.00

Three Leonard catalogs 60.00

MEISSELBACH

Fishing Reels & Landing Nets catalog: circa 1905 . . . . 75.00

MILLS, WILLIAM & SON

Circa 1880 catalog: With early rods and equipment . . 375.00

Fishing Tackle catalog: 1938 . . . . 50.00

As above: 1940 . . . . 40.00

OLD TOWN CANOE

Old Town Canoes & Boats: 1956 catalog 18.00

PARKER BROTHERS

Parker Gun Co. jobbers price list: 1878 . . . . 105.00

As above: 1936 . . . . 175.00

PAYNE, E.F.

E.F. Payne Co. Rod Catalog: circa 1930 . . . . 400.00

As above: 1951 . . . .   450.00

As above: 1977 . . . .   25.00

PERCY TACKLE COMPANY
Percy's Flies: circa 1941 16-page catalog 25.00

PFLUEGER
Fishing Tackle: 1940 catalog, 244 pages 45.00

SHAKESPEARE, WILLIAM
Tackle Catalog: 1909 catalog, 64 pages 120.00

SOUTH BEND
Fish & Feel Fit: Tackle catalog, 1935 . . . .   30.00

As above: 1937 . . . .   30.00

Fishing–What Tackle & When: 1949 . . . .   22.00

THOMAS, F.E.
Thomas Rod Co. catalog: 1955 . . . .   70.00

VOM HOFE, EDWARD & COMPANY
Edward vom Hofe & Co. catalog: 1912 . . . .   70.00

As above: 1917 . . . .   190.00

As above: 1919 . . . .   70.00

As above: 1925 . . . .   115.00

As above: 1929 . . . .   45.00

WALKER, ARTHUR & SON
Trout Reel Catalog: 1972, four pages 125.00

WINCHESTER

Winchester Arms Catalog: 1892 . . . .   275.00

As above: 1896 . . . .   265.00

Salesman's 1905 leather-bound catalog 240.00

Fishing Tackle catalog: 1933 . . . .   100.00

WINSTON ROD COMPANY

January 1974 Catalog: 24 pages, with the 1977
catalog 12.00

WRIGHT & MC GILL

Quality Fishing Tackle catalog: 1963, 60 pages 12.00

YOUNG, PAUL

More Fishing — Less Fussing catalog: 1935 . . . .   50.00

As above: circa 1952 . . . .   45.00

ZWARG, OTTO

Custom Built Reels catalog: With letter to Leon
Thomas 175.00

REPRODUCTIONS

*With today's "wonderful" copy machines fakes are easier to pro-
duce than ever. Watch your step and know the seller.*

MAGAZINES

Several reviewers and a number of readers of my original *Price Guide* lamented the absense of a chapter on old and collectible magazines and periodicals. I was remiss and hasten to correct the situation herewith. These long-ago publications are indeed part of our sporting heritage and serve collectors with an array of editorial and advertising interests.

Old magazines and periodicals can identify an old fishing lure or oddball gadject that was on the market for only one or two years. They can set or confirm introductory dates for a wide variety of sporting merchandise, provide perhaps the only illustration of a collectible, and, from an entirely different point of view, give today's sportsmen and collectors a real insight to another time that has been termed "The Golden Age of American sport."

Looking through a November 1891 *Shooting and Fishing* issue, I found an article relating the sorry condition of New England grouse and proposing that the time for regulation was at hand. Another lengthy article described a three-day live pigeon shoot between J. L. Brewer and E.D. Fulford at the Jersey City Heights grounds in Marion, New Jersey. At the end of the three days, after each contestant had shot at 300 live birds, the score was tied at 294 apiece. A shoot-off was held in which Brewer shot 25 straight while Fulford missed one bird to end up with a 24. No wonder people collect old magazines and periodicals.

Another publication that proves the point is a 1937 edition of *The Sportsman* (where my father served as the advertising manager for

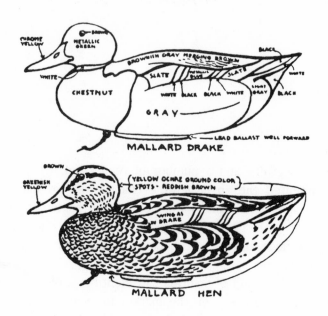

LYNN BOGUE HUNT'S detailed drawings and instructions for making duck decoys are a Hunt collector's dream come true. This rare find is from a 1906 copy of *Outing*.

most of its illustrious decade) that has a cover by Carl Burger, articles by Howard Walden II and Ben East, illustrations by Ogden Pleissner and Ralph Boyer, and Colonel H.P. Sheldon's "Guns and Game" column as its close. Need I say more?

Old sporting magazines and periodicals are hard to find. I come across them at flea markets and yard sales, where they are usually reasonably priced, and in antique shops, where costs increase dramatically. Certain old magazines command top dollar: the 1932 *Fortune*, with an article about Joel Barber; other copies of both *Fortune* and *Gentry* that feature fly fishing stories; and early copies of almost all such publications in very good condition are expensive. As is the case with all sporting collectibles, cost is driven by age coupled with supply and demand. The following prices were listed as retail costs in 1992.

American Rifleman
    1923–1926 . . . . 10.00 each
    1927–1930 . . . . 7.50
    1931–1939 . . . . 3.50
    1940–1946 . . . . 2.50
    1947–to date 2.00

Arms & Man: Predecessor to *American Rifleman*
    1906–1923 . . . . scarce

BEGINNING IN 1885

Arms & Man *(properly Arms and the Man) was, as stated, the forerunner of* American Rifleman. *It in turn was preceded by* The Rifle *(1885–1887) and* Shooting and Fishing *(1888–1906). Original publications of all of these are scarce, but reissues are available in bound volumes.*

Decoy Magazine: Formerly Decoy World Magazine
    1980–to date . . . . 4.00 each

Decoy World Magazine
    1974–1979 . . . . 2.50

North American Decoy Magazine
    1967 . . . . 35.00 each
    1968–1971 . . . . 25.00
    1972 . . . . 15.00
    1973: Winter and spring issues 10.00
           Summer and fall issues 20.00
    1974: Fall and winter issues 10.00
           Spring and summer issues 20.00

1975: Winter issue 3.00
      Summer issue 10.00
      Spring and fall issues 20.00
1976 .... 20.00
1977 .... 3.00
1978: Spring issue 15.00
      Summer, fall, and winter issues 3.00
1979 .... 3.00
1980 none issued
1981 .... 9.00
1982 .... 9.00
1983 none issued
1984: annual 9.00

MORE DECOYS

Other decoy publications include: Ward Foundation News; Decoy Hunter; Toller Trader; North American Decoy Trader; *and Hal Sorenson's now rare* Decoy Collectors Guide.

Field & Stream

1895–1900 .... 20.00
1901–1910 .... 17.50
1911–1919 .... 15.00
1920–1929 .... 10.00
1930–1945 .... 7.50
1946–1950 .... 5.00
1951–1959 .... 3.00
1960 to date 2.50

Note: Copies of *Field & Stream* with Lynn Bogue Hunt art and/or covers command higher prices as do those with art by Edwin Megargee and A. Lassel Ripley.

Forest and Stream
Prices for *Field & Stream* are applicable.

Fly Fisherman Magazine

May 1969: Vol I, No. 1	125.00
August 1969	50.00
October 1969 to April 1970	10.00
June 1970 to May 1971	7.50
Volume III: No. 1–6	5.00
Volume IV: No. 1–6	5.00
Volume V: No. 1 to date	3.00

Gray's Sporting Journal

Fall 1975 to date	7.50 each

Gun Digest

1944: No. 1	150.00
As above: Second printing	35.00
1946	100.00
1947	150.00
1949	150.00
1951–1954	40.00
1955–1956	30.00
1957–1960	15.00
1961–1967	12.50
1968 to date	10.00

Gun Dog

Vol. 1: No. 1	35.00
No. 2	30.00
No. 3–5	25.00 each
No. 6	20.00
Vol 2: No. 1–6	15.00 each
Vol 3: No. 1–2	10.00 each

	No. 3–4	7.50 each
	No. 5	15.00
	No. 6	7.50
Vol 4:	No. 1–3	15.00 each
	No. 4	5.00
	No. 5–6	10.00 each
Vol 5:	No. 1 to date	3.00 each

Guns

January 1955: Vol. I–No. 1	10.00
1955	5.00
1956 to date	3.00

Guns & Ammo

1958	5.00 each
1959 to date	3.00

Gun World Magazine

1960 to date	2.00 each

BOUND VOLUMES

Many magazines and periodicals were available in bound volumes from the publishers and many others have been bound by private collectors. Not only are bound volumes very desirable, but they transcend the market from "just" magazines to valuable books in the process.

Hunting & Fishing
See *Field & Stream* listing for prices.

Outdoor Life
See *Field & Stream* listing for prices.

Outdoors
> See *Field & Stream* listing for prices.

Outer's Recreation
> All issues . . . . 3.00 to 5.00

Shooting Times
> 1960–1961 . . . . 3.00
> 1962 to date 2.00

Note: Issues of *Shooting Times* that featured articles on double-barrel shotguns in 1961 and 1962 command higher prices.

Sporting Classics
> Volume I–No. 1 . . . . 50.00
> No. 2 1981 . . . . 15.00
> No. 3 1981 . . . . 15.00
> No. 4 1982 . . . . 35.00
> No. 5 1982 . . . . 15.00
> No. 6 1982 . . . . 10.00
> Vol. II–No. 1 . . . . 4.00
> No. 2–No. 5 . . . . 15.00
> Vol. III–No. 1 to date 4.00

Note: Volume 4–No. 1 (January-February 1986) commands a higher price.

Sports Afield
> See listing under *Field & Stream* for prices.

BEGINNING IN 1829

The first American sporting periodical was the American Turf Register and Sporting Magazine, *which first saw the light of day in 1829. Others quickly followed in the 1830s with* Spirit of the Times, New York Sporting Magazine, *and* United States Sporting Magazine *leading the way.*

The Sportsman
1927–1937 . . . .   15.00 to 20.00

Note: Several issues command much higher prices.

Stoeger's Shooter's Bible
1931 . . . .   60.00
Reprint of above 10.00
1934 . . . .   40.00
1935 . . . .   60.00
1939: World's Fair issue 75.00
1940–1941 . . . .   50.00
1942–1947 . . . .   40.00
1948 . . . .   30.00
1949 . . . .   25.00
1950–1952 . . . .   15.00
1953–1960 . . . .   10.00
1961 to date 7.50

This listing ends here, but the market truly knows no end. There are myriad sporting publications and "men's magazines" such as *Argosy, Esquire,* and *True* that deserve your consideration, as do magazines such as the aforementioned *Fortune* and *Gentry* for special-interest articles. This listing can only serve as an outline — a retail price guide to a few sporting publications that have proved both popular and available. And last, but certainly not least, I owe Lou Rajek a heartfelt thank you for making what might have been an impossible task manageable. His Highwood Bookshop in Traverse City, Michigan, stocks more than 100,000 sporting magazines. Give him a shout; chances are he has what you want.

SPORTING BOOKS

Two years ago when I wrote my first *Price Guide,* no one could have predicted the length and depth of the recession of the early 1990s nor could anyone have had any idea that fine sporting books would shine in an otherwise dull marketplace — but that is exactly what has transpired. Fishing books have done particularly well, but all sporting books have proved steady performers in a shaky time for other sporting antiques and collectibles. Condition, as always, was a prime consideration. And before we get on to prices and other aspects of sporting book collecting, you should study the tough standards booksellers set for themselves. You cannot compete without the proper "tools," and these are basic.

CONDITION DESCRIPTION

Mint: *Should only be used to describe books that are as-issued, complete with dust jacket if issued with one, in perfect condition.*

Fine: *Near to the above without being "crisp." A dust jacket can have minor wear.*

Very Good: *Shows some wear, but no tears or other blemishes. Any defects should be noted.*

Good: *An average used book, showing use, but with all pages and leaves present. Defects should be noted.*

Fair: *Has all of its text pages but may have other defects.*

Poor: *A reading copy that has no other merit. Do not confuse a reading copy with a "binding copy," which is one with fine leaves but a poor or nonexistent binding.*

The strength of the 1990s sporting book market should not have come as a surprise to this writer, who knows full well that these treasured volumes are getting harder and harder to come by. But, in truth, it did. Sporting books continue to be fine long-term invest-ments and I shall never doubt their enduring joy and value again and neither should you. Further proof of this long-term monetary truth is evidenced by a comparison of 1971-1991 price changes that I recently compiled with the kind cooperation of the Angler's and Shooter's Bookshelf in Goshen, Connecticut. I think it speaks for itself.

1971–1991

A SCORE OF APPRECIATION

In 1971 a fine copy of the Derrydale Press' Tales of a Big Game Guide *by Russell Annabel sold for $65.00. Today it is a bargain at $375.00. In 1971 Babcock's* My Health is Better In November *was $17.50. Today it sells for $125.00. Bates'* Atlantic Salmon Flies and Fishing *was new in 1971 and went for $14.95. Today it brings $125.00.*

Other books (with the 1971 price first and today's price second) in-clude: Gunner's Dawn *by Roland Clark; $75.00 and $750.00;* Connett's Random Casts, *$50.00 and $250.00; Zane Grey's* Tales of Fishing Virgin Seas, *$22.50 and $200.00, and his* Tales of Fishes *at $17.00 and $85.00; Haig-Brown's* Fisherman's Spring, *$8.50 and $60.00; Ray Holland's* Scattergunning, *$12.50 and $75.00; and Ed Zern's* To Hell With Fishing, *$6.50 and $20.00. And the list goes on and on and on.*

The following list of sporting books is arranged alphabetically by author. None of the titles from my first *Price Guide* are repeated here and if the book or author you are looking for is not listed, I suggest you refer to the earlier volume.

SPORTING BOOKS from the Samuel B. Webb library auction by William Doyle include Titian Peale's copy of Edwin James's *Account of an Expedition to the Rocky Mountains* and William Beebe's *A Monograph of the Pheasants*. Photograph courtesy of William Doyle Galleries, New York.

IMPORTANT ABBREVIATIONS

There are several common bookseller abbreviations you should know and that I use in this chapter. Dj *means dust jacket,* pp *means privately printed,* nd *stands for no date of publication,* np *for no place,* ep *is endpaper,* ffep *means free front endpaper,* teg *signifies that top edges are gilt,* s/n *is signed and numbered, and* aeg *tells you that all edges are so treated.*

ABBEY, EDWARD

Desert Solitude: New York 1968. Illustrated by
Peter Parnell. (first edition) 50.00

ALDAM, W. H.

*A Quaint Treatise on "Flee, and the Art of Artyfichall
Flee Making"*: London 1876 . . . .   1,200.00

As above: 1875 (first edition) 1,750.00

ALEXANDER, KIRKLAND

The Log of The North Shore Club: New York 1911.
Very good ex-library copy 50.00

ANDERSON, CHARLES J.

Lake Ngami: New York 1857. Second printing of
the American edition. Good 75.00

ANDERSON, KENNETH

The Black Panther of Sivanipalli: Chicago 1960. A
fine copy of the first edition 30.00

ANDERSON, LUTHER

How to Hunt Deer and Small Game: New York
1959. Fine first edition with dust jacket (dj) 12.00

How to Hunt Whitetail Deer: New York 1968. First
edition in a fine dust jacket 12.00

Hunting, Fishing, & Camping New York 1945. A
fine copy of the first edition with dj 12.00

Hunting the Woodlands for Small & Big Game: San
Diego 1980. Very good with good dj 12.00

ARNOLD, RICHARD

The Shooter's Handbook: London 1955. A very good
copy of the first edition 17.50

Pigeon Shooting: London 1956. A fine copy of a
hard-to-find title 18.00

Automatic & Repeating Shotguns: New York 1960.
A fine copy in a very good dj 24.00

BABCOCK, LOUIS L.

The Tarpon: Fifth edition limited to 250 signed and
numbered copies. Very scarce 275.00

BABCOCK, PHILIP H.

Falling Leaves: Derrydale 1937. Limited to 950
signed and numbered copies 200.00

Back Then: Wautoma 1989. New 25.00

BABSON, STANLEY M.

Bonefishing: New York 1965. A very good copy of
the first edition with dj 40.00

BAY, KENNETH

Salt Water Flies: Philadelphia 1972. A fine copy of
the first edition with dj 30.00

The American Fly Tier's Handbook: New York 1979.
A fine first edition with fine dj 30.00

BRIGGS, ELLIS O.

Shots Heard Round the World: New York 1957. A
fine copy of the first edition with a good dj 35.00

Another copy. Good 15.00

BROOKS, CHARLES E.

Larger Trout for the Western Fly Fisherman: New
York 1972. Second printing. Scarce. Fine with dj 45.00

The Living River: New York 1979. First edition in
fine condition with fine dj 30.00

Nymph Fishing For Larger Trout: New York 1976.
First printing in fine condition 45.00

The Trout & The Stream: New York 1974. A fine
first edition of a scarce book with dj 50.00

Another as above, second printing 30.00

BROWNE, CHARLES

The Gun Club Cookbook: New York 1934. Revised
edition in good condition 15.00

CAMP, SAMUEL G.

Taking Trout With The Dry Fly: New York 1930. A
very good first edition in a good dj 24.00

Fishing Kits and Equipment: New York 1923. A
very good reprint 10.00

The Fine Art of Fishing: New York 1936. A fine
copy of the *Outing* reprint 22.50

The Angler's Handbook: Columbus 1925. A very
good copy 10.00

CAUCCI, AL AND NASTASI, BOB

Hatches: New York 1975. A very good copy in a
good dust jacket 30.00

Hatches II: New York 1990. A mint reprint in a mint
dust jacket 33.00

Fly-Tyer's Color Guide: New York 1978. First
edition in very fine condition with dj 35.00

CLARK, JAMES L.

Trails of the Hunted: Boston 1928. A very good
copy of the first printing 50.00

CLEVELAND, GROVER

Fishing & Shooting Sketches: A & F New York. A
reprint of the 1906 edition. Very fine 30.00

COX, CHARLES E., JR.

John Tobias — Sportsman: Derrydale 1937. Limited
edition of 950, signed, fine 130.00

CROWE, JOHN

The Book of Trout Lore: New York 1947. A very
good copy of the first edition with dj 30.00

Another: Spine faded 20.00

DAVIS, EDMUND W.

Salmon Fishing on The Grand Cascapedia. pp 1904.
One of only 100 copies. Fine 1,300.00

DAVIS, S. T.

Caribou Shooting in New Foundland: Lancaster
1895. A very good copy of a scarce book 150.00

Another as above 150.00

DOYLE, A. CONAN

Lone Dhow: New York 1964. First American edition
of an unusual book 25.00

EATON, ELON HOWARD

Birds of New York: Albany 1910-14. Two-volume
first edition in very good condition 150.00

ELDER, FRANK

The Book of The Hackle: Edinburgh nd. A mint copy
of this fly tyer's guide with dj 20.00

ENDICOTT, WENDELL

Adventures in Alaska & Along The Trail: New York
1928. Signed first edition in very good condition 85.00

Another as above 50.00

ETCHEN, FRED

Common Sense Shotgun Shooting: Huntington 1964.
A fine copy of this important volume 24.00

EVANS, GEORGE BIRD

An Affair With Grouse: Clinton 1982. One of 1,000
signed and numbered copies. As new 225.00

The Bird Dog Book: Clinton 1979. One of 1,000 s/n
copies. As new in slipcase 250.00

Recollections of a Shooting Guest: Clinton 1978. One
of 1,000 s/n copies. As new 225.00

The Upland Gunner's Book: Clinton 1979. One of
1,000 s/n copies. Very fine in slipcase 175.00

The Woodcock Book: Clinton 1977. One of 1,000 s/n
copies. As new 350.00

The Ruffed Grouse Book: Clinton 1977. One of 1,000
s/n copies. As new 350.00

Grouse Along The Tramroad: pp. One of 1,500
signed and numbered copies 125.00

Nash Buckingham's Letters to John Bailey: pp. One
of 575 numbered copies. Signed. As new 125.00

George Bird Evans Introduces: pp. One of 1,150 s/n
copies. As new 45.00

The Upland Shooting Life: New York 1971. The
scarce, true, first edition. Signed. Fine with dj 75.00

The Best of Nash Buckingham: New York 1973. The
first edition of this popular book. Fine with dj 45.00

FAULKNER, WILLIAM

Big Woods: New York 1955. The first edition of this
scarce title. Very fine with dj 100.00

FOA, EDOUARD

After Big Game in Central Africa: Long Beach 1986.
Reprint of 1899 edition. Mint 45.00

FORBUSH, EDWARD H.

Important American Game Birds: DuPont 1917.
Illustrations by Lynn Bogue Hunt. Paperbound 75.00

Useful Birds & Their Protection: Boston nd. Good
ex-library copy 5.00

*A History of the Gamebirds, Wildfowl and Shorebirds
of Massachusetts*: Boston 1912 . . . .   75.00

Another as above 35.00

Portraits of New England Birds: Boston 1932. The
plate volume for the above history 70.00

FOOTE, JOHN TAINTOR

Angler's All: New York 1947. A fine copy of
collected tales. Dust jacket 50.00

Blister Jones: Indianapolis 1913. Fine copy of the
author's first book 65.00

Broadway Angler: New York 1937. First edition of
popular title with a dust jacket 40.00

Change of Idols: New York 1935. A very fine copy
with a good dust jacket 40.00

Another: Good 30.00

Daughter of Delilah: New York 1936. First edition
with a good dj 40.00

Fatal Gesture: New York 1933. First printing in
very fine condition with dj 45.00

Jing: Derrydale 1938. One of 950 numbered copies
illustrated by A. L. Ripley 100.00

The Number One Boy: New York 1926. First edition
of a scarce title. Fine 45.00

THE SPORTING BOOKPLATE OF
SAMUEL B. WEBB is a valued addition
to a sporting book. His library was sold
by William Doyle Galleries in 1991.

The Song of The Dragon: New York 1923. Very
scarce first printing. Very good 50.00

Trub's Diary: New York 1928. Hard to find edition
(not first) in very good condition 30.00

The Wedding Gift: New York 1924. First edition of
this popular book. Very good 40.00

IS SOMEONE MISSING?

*If the author or book you are looking for is not here, you may find it
in my first* Price Guide, *which remains in print and available
from your bookseller or from the publisher, whose address is listed
elsewhere in this volume.*

FORESTER, FRANK

The Complete Manual For Young Sportsmen: New
York 1856. A very good copy of the first edition 75.00

Another: 1868 . . . .   60.00

Fish & Fishing In The United States: London 1849.
Covers are good, internally fine 150.00

Sporting Scenes & Sundry Sketches: New York 1842.
Two-volume first edition. Very good 200.00

Field Sports of The United States: New York 1849.
Two-volume first edition. Very fine 180.00

The Sporting Novels of Frank Forester. Derrydale
1930. Four volumes. Limited to 750 sets. Very fine .   275.00

The Dog: New York 1873. A fine copy 80.00

FRANCIS, AUSTIN M.

Catskill Rivers: New York 1983. Deluxe edition
limited to 300 numbered and signed copies. As new .   250.00

As above. The first trade edition 28.00

FRANK, CHARLES W., JR.

Louisiana Duck Decoys: Gretna 1979. Second
printing (first was paperbound) of this important
book 50.00

GALLICO, PAUL

The Snow Goose: New York 1941. The first edition
of this classic story. Fine with dj 30.00

GATES, ELGIN T.

Trophy Hunter In Asia: New York 1971. Very fine
in a very fine dj 100.00

GERLACH, REX

Creative Fly Tying & Fly Fishing: New York 1974.
Very fine with dj 25.00

Fly Fishing For Rainbows: Harrisburg 1988. As new
with fine dj 20.00

GOOCH, BOB

Coveys & Singles: San Diego 1980. First edition
with dj. As new 12.00

In Search of The Wild Turkey: Waukegan 1978.
Very fine with fine dust jacket 20.00

Squirrels & Squirrel Hunting: Cambridge 1972.
Very fine with fine dj 7.50

The Weedy World of The Pickerels: South Brunswick
1970. Very fine with dj 20.00

GRISWOLD, FRANK GRAY

Fish Facts & Fancies: Norwood 1923. A signed copy
in very good condition 75.00

Fish Facts & Fancies: (Volume II) Norwood 1925. A
very good signed copy 75.00

Another: The above books combined in one volume by
Scribners 1926. Limited to 1,000 copies 45.00

The Memoirs of a Salmon: Norwood 1931. Inscribed
and signed copy. Fine 50.00

Observations on a Salmon River: pp 1922. A fine
signed copy 125.00

Salmo Salar: Norwood 1929. A very good copy
signed by the author 90.00

Another: As above, fine but not signed 90.00

HALFORD, FREDERIC M.

Dry Fly Entomology: London 1897. The first edition
with hand-colored plates 150.00

As above: The deluxe edition limited to 100 with
volume of flies in sunken mounts 1,700.00

Dry Fly Fishing in Theory & Practice: London 1889.
Some wear 150.00

The Dry Fly Man's Handbook: London 1913. The
first edition 140.00

Floating Flies & How To Dress Them: London 1886.
Ninety hand-colored flies in nine plates 300.00

Modern Development of the Dry Fly: London 1910.
The first edition with moderate wear 140.00

HALL, HENRY M.

A Gathering of Shore Birds: New York 1960. The
first edition in fine condition with dj 40.00

The Ruffed Grouse: New York 1946. First edition in
very good condition with dj 40.00

Woodcock Ways: New York 1946. First edition with
minor wear and dj 38.00

HAMMOND, S. T.

My Friend The Partridge: New York 1908. First
edition of a scarce book in very good condition 100.00

Hitting vs Missing with The Shotgun: New York
1900. Very good copy 20.00

HAZELTON, WILLIAM C.

Fred Kimble: Master Duck Shot of The World:
Chicago 1923. First edition of a very rare book 850.00

Duck Shooting & Hunting Sketches: Chicago 1916. A
fine copy of a scarce title 250.00

Tales of Duck & Goose Shooting: Chicago 1916. A
fine copy of a hard-to-find volume 220.00

HEWITT, EDWARD R.

Days From Seventy-Five to Ninety: New York 1957.
First edition of a scarce title. Very fine 120.00

Good Land From Poor Soil: Trenton 1951. A fine
copy with inscribed letter laid in 120.00

Another: Good 40.00

Hewitt's Handbook of Fly Fishing: New York 1933.
A fine copy 50.00

Hewitt's Handbook of Stream Improvement: New
York 1934. A fine signed copy 110.00

Hewitt's Nymph Fly Fishing: New York 1935. A
very fine copy of this small volume 50.00

Secrets of The Salmon: New York 1925. A signed
and inscribed first trade edition. Fine 90.00

HOLDER, CHARLES

Life In The Open: New York 1906. A very good
copy of the first edition 40.00

The Log of The Sea Angler: New York 1906. A good
copy of the first edition 45.00

IRVING, WASHINGTON

The Angler: pp Portland 1931. Limited to 150 s/n
copies. Very good 100.00

The Angler: pp New York 1933. Limited to 180
copies. Signed presentation copy 80.00

JACKSON, JOHN

The Practical Fly-Fisher: London 1854. A very good
copy of the rare first edition 650.00

Another: 1862 second edition 300.00

JONES, BURT

Habits, Haunts, and Antecdotes of The Moose: PP
Boston 1901. One of 1,000 copies. Very good 75.00

JORDAN, D. S.

Fishes: New York 1907. First edition of the
condensed 1905 edition 45.00

Another: 1927 edition 25.00

Another: 1925 edition 25.00

KELSON, GEORGE

The Salmon Fly: Goshen 1979. Facsimile of the
1895 edition. As new 75.00

KITE, OLIVER

A Fisherman's Diary: London 1969. A fine copy of
the first edition with dj 40.00

KREH, LEFTY

Fly Fishing in Salt Water: New York 1974. A fine
copy of the first edition with dj 40.00

Another: Second printing 25.00

KREH, LEFTY & SOSIN, MARK

Practical Fishing Knots: New York 1972. A fine
copy of the first edition with dj 35.00

LATHAM, ROGER M.

Complete Book of The Wild Turkey: Harrisburg
1956. A very good signed copy of the first edition . . . 65.00

Another: 1976 edition 20.00

LEONARD, J. EDSON

The Essential Fly-Tier: Englewood 1976. A fine
copy of the first edition with dj 30.00

Flies: New York 1950. A very good signed
presentation copy of the first edition with dj 75.00

Another: Later printing(s) 25.00

Fly Rod Casting: New York 1953. The first edition.
Fine with dj 15.00

Bait Rod Casting: New York 1953. A fine copy of
the first printing with dj 15.00

Feather In The Breeze: New York 1974. A mint copy
of the first edition 20.00

LIND, JAMES A.

Muskie!: Chicago 1964. Signed presentation copy of
an important book. Fine with dj 110.00

LUCAS, JASON

Lucas on Bass Fishing: New York 1947. A very
good copy of the first edition 30.00

Another: Revised 1949 edition 30.00

Another: Revised (again) 1962 edition 30.00

"NEW YORK PRICES"

Not long ago I overheard a man who was thumbing through a copy of my first Price Guide *tell his companion that it contained "New York prices." I could only assume he meant that the prices were high, but I didn't speak. I wouldn't tell him, but I will tell you: The prices in the* Price Guides *come from a variety of booksellers and book auctions across the United States including — I must admit — the state of New York.*

MAASS, DAVID & HILL, GENE

A Gallery of Waterfowl & Upland Birds: Los
Angeles 1978. A s/n copy of the limited edition 300.00

Another: Trade edition 100.00

MAC DOWELL, SYL

Western Trout: New York (Borzoi) 1948. A fine
copy of the first edition with dj 35.00

MARSH, BRIAN

The Last Trophy: New York 1982. A fine copy of the
first edition with dj 25.00

MATHER, FRED

In Louisiana Lowlands: New York 1900. A very
good copy of this scarce title 160.00

MEGARGEE, EDWIN

Dogs: New York 1942. A very good copy of the first
edition 40.00

Gun Dogs At Work: New York 1945. A fine copy of
illustrated history. Paperbound 12.00

The Dog Dictionary: Cleveland 1954. A fine copy of
the first edition with dj 40.00

MERWIN, JOHN

Stillwater Trout: New York 1980. A very good copy
of the first printing with dj 15.00

MEYER, JERRY

The Sporting Clays Handbook: New York 1990. A
mint copy of this popular book 30.00

MILLAIS, J. G.

Life of Frederick Courtnay Selous DSO: London
1919. Second printing. Very good 100.00

Newfoundland & Its Untrodden Ways: New York
(A&F) 1967. Reprint of 1907 edition. Mint 40.00

MINER, JACK

Jack Miner & The Birds: Toronto 1923. A very good
signed copy of the first edition 35.00

NEWHOUSE, S.

The Trapper's Guide: Oneida 1865. A scarce first
edition of a fragile paperbound book 75.00

NORRIS, CHARLES G.

Eastern Upland Shooting: Philadelphia 1946. A very
good copy of the first edition 55.00

Another: Reprint of the above. Mint 35.00

OLSEN, SIGURD F.

Wilderness Days: New York 1972. Second edition in
fine condition with dj 15.00

Open Horizons: New York 1969. A fine copy with a
fine dj 15.00

Runes of The North: New York 1963. A mint copy of
the first edition 35.00

ORMOND, CLYDE

Bear: Harrisburg 1961. A mint copy in a repaired dj . .   20.00

Complete Book of Hunting: New York 1962. A mint
copy 20.00

Complete Book of Outdoor Lore: New York 1964.
Mint with fine dj 20.00

Hunting Our Biggest Game: Harrisburg 1956. A
scarce title in very fine condition with dj 25.00

Hunting Our Medium Sized Game: Harrisburg
1958. A mint copy 25.00

Outdoorsman's Handbook: New York 1970. A mint
copy 20.00

Hunting In The Northwest: New York (Borzoi)
1948. A fine copy of the first edition with worn dj . . .   40.00

ORTEGAY GASSET, JOSE

Meditations on Hunting: New York 1972. First
English translation. Fine with dj 130.00

Another: Mint 150.00

OSBOURNE, EDWARD B.

> *Letters From The Woods*: Poughkeepsie 1893. A
> very good copy of a very scarce book 120.00

PALMER, C. H.

> *The Salmon Rivers of Newfoundland*: Boston 1928.
> A scarce first edition. Fine with dj 75.00

PEACH, ARTHUR W.

> *The Country Rod & Gun Book*: Countryman 1938. A
> fine copy of the first edition with dj 25.00

PELL, STUYVESANT M.

> *Scribblings of an Outdoor Boy*: pp Princeton 1945. A
> very good copy of a scarce book 80.00

PRICE, TAFF

> *The Angler's Sedge*: London 1989. A mint copy
> about fishing with the sedge, caddis, etc 24.00

RILING, RAY

> *Guns & Shooting*: Greenberg 1951. One of 1,500
> copies of the original bibliography. Fine 175.00

RIPLEY, A. LASSELL

> *Paintings*: Barre 1972. A very fine copy of a limited
> edition (1,500) 175.00

> *Sporting Etchings*: Barre 1970. A very fine slipcased
> copy of a limited edition (500) 175.00

> *Another*: As above. Trade edition 40.00

ROBB, JAMES

Notable Angling Literature: London nd. A very good
copy of this bibliography 55.00

ROBINSON, BEN C.

Pond, Lake & Stream Fishing: Philadelphia 1941. A
very good copy with dj 12.50

Woodland, Field, & Waterfowl Shooting. Philadelphia
1946. A very good copy with dj 12.50

RUE, LEONARD LEE

Gamebirds of North America: New York 1973. A
very good copy with dj 15.00

Cottontail: New York 1965. A good copy 5.00

The World of the Ruffed Grouse: Philadelphia 1973.
A fine copy with dj. First edition 25.00

Complete Guide to Game Animals: New York 1981.
The second revised edition. Very good with dj 10.00

The World of the Whitetailed Deer: Philadelphia
1962. A mint copy 15.00

ST. JOHN, LARRY

Practical Bait Casting: New York 1932. A fine copy . .   12.50

Practical Fly Fishing: New York 1920. A fine copy
of the scarce first edition 27.50

SALMON, RICHARD

Fly Fishing For Trout: New York 1952. A fine copy
of a scarce book with dj 85.00

SAMSON, JACK

The Bear Book: Clinton 1982. The second edition in
mint condition 30.00

Hunting The Southwest: Clinton 1983. A mint copy
in a fine slipcase 35.00

Line Down: New York 1974. A very fine copy of the
first edition with dj 25.00

The Sportsman's World: New York 1976. A fine
copy with dj 20.00

SCHULLERY, PAUL

American Fly Fishing: New York 1987. A first
edition signed by the author. Very fine 75.00

Another: Not signed 65.00

SCOTT, GENIO C.

Fishing in American Waters: New York 1869.
Scarce first edition in very good condition 90.00

Another: 1875 edition. Good 45.00

SCOTT, PETER

A Coloured Ket To the Waterfowl: New York 1961.
The scarce hardbound edition 25.00

A Thousand Geese: Boston 1954. A very fine copy
of the first American edition 25.00

The Eye of The Wind: Boston 1961. A fine copy of
this autobiography 35.00

Morning Flight: London 1935. One of 750 s/n
copies. Very fine with dj 550.00

Wild Chorus: London 1938. One of 1,250 s/n
copies. Very fine with dj 500.00

CONDITION • CONDITION • CONDITION

I may harp on many things, but the condition of books — particularly rare, expensive books — is of prime importance and even a minor flaw will reduce value.

SELL, FRANCIS E.

Advanced Hunting on Deer & Elk Trails: Harrisburg 1954. A fine first edition with dj 40.00

The Deer Hunter's Guide: Harrisburg 1964. A very good copy of the first printing with dj 18.00

Small Game Hunting: 1955. The first edition in fine condition with dj 18.00

The American Deer Hunter: Harrisburg 1957. A fine copy of the second printing 40.00

Practical Fresh Water Fishing: Harrisburg 1960. A mint copy with so-so dust jacket 30.00

SETON-THOMPSON, ERNEST

Wild Animals I Have Known: New York 1942. Reprint of the original 1898 edition 15.00

Woodland Tales: New York 1925. A fine copy 20.00

Bannertail: New York 1922. A very good copy of the first printing 60.00

The Arctic Prairies: London 1912. The first British edition. Fine 90.00

Another: Later printing 55.00

Lives of The Hunted: New York 1901. A fine copy of the first edition 25.00

Bird Portraits: Boston 1901. A fine copy of a scarce
title 100.00

The Book of Woodcraft: New York 1921. A very fine
copy 35.00

Krag & Johnny Bear: New York 1912. A scarce
book in very fine condition 50.00

Two Little Savages: New York 1903. Another scarce
title. Fine 35.00

Rolf in the Woods: New York 1917. A fine copy of a
hard-to-find book 30.00

Monarch — The Bear of Tallac: New York 1904. A
fine first edition 25.00

SHEPARD, ODELL

The Harvest of a Quiet Eye: Boston 1927. A very
good copy of the first edition 25.00

Thy Rod & Thy Creel: Hartford 1930. A very good
inscribed copy of the first edition 100.00

SHEPPERSON, A. B.

An Angler's Anthology: Charlottesville 1932. A very
good copy of a scarce book 60.00

SMEDLEY, HAROLD H.

Fly Patterns & Their Origins: Muskegon 1943. The
scarce first edition signed and with dj 200.00

Another: The fourth revised edition 85.00

More Fly Patterns: Muskegon 1944. A scarce book
in very good condition 100.00

Trout of Michigan: Michigan 1938. A very fine copy
of a very scarce book 100.00

Accuracy Fly Casting: New York 1949. A fine copy
of this volume 30.00

SMITH, BRIAN R.

Samworth Books, A Descriptive Bibliography: 1990.
An important title for the collector 50.00

SNYDER, HARRY M.

Snyder's Book of Big Game Hunting: New York
1950. A very fine copy with dj 50.00

Another: A very good copy with dj 40.00

STEVENS, CHARLES W.

Fishing in Maine Lakes: Boston 1881. A very good
copy of a scarce title 85.00

STODDART, THOMAS T.

The Bobwhite Quail: New York 1931. One of 260
s/n copies with Benson fronts. Fine 1,000.00

Another: 1932 trade edition. Fine 175.00

TALLEUR, RICHARD

Fishing For Trout: New York 1974. A fine signed
copy of the first edition with dj 35.00

Another: As above, not signed 25.00

The Fly-Tyer's Primer: Piscataway 1986. A fine,
signed first edition with tipped-in fly 50.00

The Versatile Fly-Tyer: New York 1990. A fine copy
of the first edition with dj 35.00

TAYLOR, WALTER P.

The Deer of North America: Harrisburg 1969. A fine
copy of the fourth edition 50.00

THOMPSON, J. M.

The Witchery of Archery: New York 1879. A good
copy of the second edition 100.00

Another: 1928 revised edition. Fine 75.00

TINKER, S. W.

Hawaiian Fishes: Honolulu 1944. A fine copy of a
scarce volume 100.00

Another: A very good copy 50.00

TINSLEY, J. B.

The Sailfish: Florida 1964. One of 500 s/n copies.
Mint, in slipcase 150.00

TURNER, GRAHAM

Fishing Tackle: A Collector's Guide: London 1989.
First edition. As new 75.00

VAN WORMER, JOE

The World of The Black Bear: Philadelphia 1966. A
mint copy of the first edition 20.00

The World of The Canada Goose: Philadelphia 1968.
A mint copy of the second printing 15.00

VENIARD, JOHN

A Further Guide to Fly Dressing: London 1980. A
mint copy 27.50

Reservoir & Lake Flies: London 1973. A mint copy
of this first edition with slipcase 30.00

WALKER, C. F.

The Art of Chalk Stream Fishing: London 1968. A
fine copy of the first edition 35.00

WEEKS, EDWARD

Fresh Waters: Boston 1968. A fine, signed copy
with dj 40.00

In Friendly Candor: Boston 1959. A very good first
edition with dj 20.00

The Miramichi Fish & Game Club: pp 1984. First
edition. As new 30.00

The Moise Salmon Club: Barre 1971. One of 1,500
s/n copies. Fine in slipcase 165.00

The Open Heart: Boston 1955. A very fine signed
copy with dj 35.00

WETHERELL, W. D.

Vermont River: New York 1984. A very fine copy of
the first edition 14.00

WILLIAMS, C. S.

Honker: Princeton 1967. A fine copy of a scarce
title with dj 40.00

WILSON, EUGENE E.

A Pilgrimage of Anglers: Hartford 1952. One of 50
signed copies. Fine in fine slipcase 200.00

A North Woods Rendezvous: Hartford 1953. One of
1,250 s/n copies. Fine in good slipcase 75.00

WOOLNER, FRANK

My New England: Lexington 1972. A fine copy of
the first edition 25.00

Timberdoodle: New York 1974. A fine copy of the
first edition with dj 25.00

Grouse & Grouse Hunting: New York 1974. The
fifth printing. Mint 30.00

Trout Hunting: New York 1977. A mint copy of the
first printing with dj 15.00

Modern Salt Water Sport Fishing: New York 1972.
As new with dj 25.00

GOLF À LA WOOLNER

*One of the joys of compiling a list of this type is the many fond
memories I find between the titles. Golf à la Woolner, on a putting
green at a Connecticut motel after attending a long-ago Winchester
Winner's Circle dinner, is such a memory. I do not recall who won
but I do know that the shotguns were unusually loud the next
morning.*

WRIGHT, LEONARD M., JR.

Fishing the Dry Fly as a Living Insect: New York
1972. A fine copy of the first edition 40.00
The Ways of Trout: New York 1985. A good copy
with soiled covers 15.00

YOUNG, RALPH W.

Grizzlies Don't Come Easy: Piscataway 1981. A fine
copy of the first edition 30.00

My Lost Wilderness: Piscataway 1983. A fine copy of
the first edition with dust jacket 20.00

ZOUCH, THOMAS

The Life of Issac Walton: London 1823. A very fine
copy of this scarce title 600.00

Another: a fine copy 400.00

ZUTZ, DON

The Double Shotgun: New York 1985. The revised
edition. Mint with dust jacket 30.00

FISHING LURES, PLUGS, AND SPOONS

In the first edition of my *Price Guide* I told you how far and fast fishing lures, plugs, and spoons had come from near obscurity to five-figure antiques in only fifteen years. Now I must tell you about today and venture a guess about tomorrow. Don't worry — the news is not all bad. A company in Connecticut is reproducing the popular and expensive lures of our past and — as they say — imitation is the sincerest form of flattery, proving that there are some who are still betting big bucks on these sporting collectibles.

All forms of lures, plugs, and spoons have been affected by the economic realities of the early 1990s, as have all other sporting antiques and collectibles. People are loath to invest when tomorrow is uncertain, and this has caused prices to fall. In my first *Price Guide* I used both auction and catalog prices to give you the big picture, but because of the present economy all prices listed here are for lures sold at recent auctions. Bear in mind that all of these sales were subject to a 10 percent buyer's fee that is not reflected in the listings.

The following list is in alphabetical order by maker and manufacturer. The photographs were kindly provided by Bob Lang of Raymond, Maine.

NFLCC

Everyone with an interest in old fishing lures should be a member of the National Fishing Lure Collector's Club. To find out more write NFLCC, 3835 West Addison, Chicago, Illinois, 60618. Address your inquiry to Steve Lumpkin.

ABBEY & IMBRIE

Pearl Minnow: 2 3/4" lure made from shell, in
wooden box (unmarked) 50.00

ARBOGAST

Tin Liz Snake: Paint chipping and hook barb
missing. 175.00

Weedless Tin Liz Sunfish: Has glass eyes, but is
missing tail. Otherwise mint 75.00

Framed group of twenty Tin Liz lures: Good to
excellent condition 825.00

BUEL

1852 patent spinner: A 4" lure with 3" blade, in good
condition. 375.00

CHAPMAN

Chapman & Son marked 10" spinner: With 4 1/2"
blade in excellent condition 625.00

CHAUTAUQUA

Automatic Striking Bait: 4" brass lure that sets
hooks when angler pulls. Rare 5,000.00

Handcarved Trout 300.00

Handcarved Bullhead 275.00

Handcarved muskie lure 100.00

COMSTOCK

Flying Helgramite: 1883 patent Type II metal lure
with red glass eyes. Excellent 5,000.00

As above: (Type I) with bent hooks and slight body
scratching 2,200.00

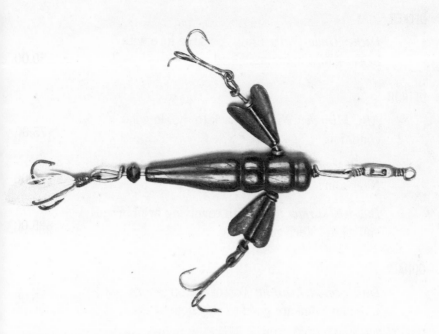

COMSTOCK FLYING HELGRAMITE (1883 Patent) is a rare and desireable lure. This one sold for $2,200 plus a 10% buyer's fee. Photograph by Bob Lang.

CREEK CHUB

Rare box of six lures: Dating from 1923-24 in very good condition throughout 850.00

Tarpon Pikie #4002: Red and white in box and as new 75.00

Baby Jigger: Frog finish with glass eyes. Near-mint condition 135.00

Husky minnow: A 5" lure in its original old yellow box 300.00

Chub Wiggler #106: As new in original box with 1917 catalog enclosed 90.00

Store display box of six Pikie 700 lures: In various colors 625.00

DECKER

Decker UnderWater Lure: A scarce lure with
heavy-gauge spinners. Good condition 250.00

DETROIT

ABC Minnow: With red back (only), in good
condition 150.00

Small Underwater Minnow: With pointed propeller.
Near-mint 400.00

Bug-type surface bait: With revolving head in red
and white. Very good 250.00

DONALY

Dealer counter carton: Top of carton is torn, six
lures included are good to excellent 2,200.00

EXPERT

Expert Minnow (so marked): With removable side
hooks. Very good condition 375.00

THE RIGHT PARTS

*Just as automobile collectors do not want plastic fenders on their
Model T and Model A vehicles, lure collectors want original parts
on their lures. Learn about hooks and hook hardware — they can
make all the difference.*

C. R. HARRIS

Harris Cork Frog: This rare lure is missing its
hanging weight, but very good 175.00

COLLECTIBLE FROG by H. R. Harris is eagerly sought by both lure and antique collectors. Photograph by Bob Lang.

RILEY HASKELL

Haskell Minnow: This 3 3/8" hollow copper lure is the finest of these rare minnows yet offered 13,000.00

Note: When one of these little darlings was sold in 1988 for $20,000 plus a $2,000 buyer's fee it set a record for any and all fishing tackle sales that is expected to stand for a long time.

HEDDON

Killer #450: A 1905-vintage lure in red and white and near-excellent condition 425.00

As above: Worn to primer. Structurally fine 175.00

#175 Minnow: In light green and white belly and hand-painted gills. Excellent 120.00

#300 Minnow: With green crackle back finish in near-excellent condition 75.00

As above: Chip on one side. Varnish flaking 70.00

Spin-Diver: 4 1/4" lure has glass eyes, white, green, and red finish, and flaking 245.00

Early Killer: With brass hardware and in
near-excellent condition 650.00

#900 Swimming Minnow: 4 1/2" with yellow body
with red and green. Very good 295.00

Dummy-Double: Early glass-eyed in original
strawberry finish. Very good 325.00

Another: Heavy hardware, green and red spots and
very good with minor chipping 400.00

Multiple Metal Minnow: This gold-finish lure is rare
and excellent 600.00

Coast Minnow: Early 2 1/2" model stripped to
original white paint 160.00

Another: In rainbow finish and showing much use.
Good condition 100.00

#100 Minnow: In marked wooden box. Lure has
chipping, box is legible 170.00

Another: Very good lure–excellent box 200.00

Bottle-Nose Tadpolly: Rainbow finish, some varnish
flaking and overcoat of varnish 100.00

Slope Nose Expert: Surface lure. Blue and white
with red collar. Very good 150.00

Another: Paint chipping and touch-up 75.00

Another: Stripped to primer 25.00

#800 Swimming Minnow: Glass eyes, hand-painted
gills, and near excellent. Rare 400.00

HOUSON

Michigan Lifelike Minnow: Green back with white
belly, with case 600.00

Another: Small size with paint checking and
cracking. Good 375.00

HOWE

Howe Vacuum Bass Bait: In original black and gold
box 300.00

K & K

K & K Animated Minnow: 4" jointed body. Has
some scrapes and missing paint 125.00

Another: Very good 250.00

Another: "Minnoette" model. Near-mint 450.00

KEELING

5" Musky Expert: Green and black with silver belly
in very good condition with display case 300.00

KENT

Kent Frog: A 2 1/2" lure with wire hooks and
propellers. Minor hook marks 650.00

LANE

Lane's Automatic Minnow: Complete with
detachable harness. Minor chips, but near excellent   1,700.00

Wagtail Wobbler: 3 7/8" size in brown and gold. A
few minor chips 125.00

Another 4 1/8" size: Very good 175.00

As above 175.00

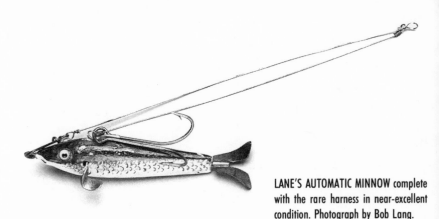

LANE'S AUTOMATIC MINNOW complete with the rare harness in near-excellent condition. Photograph by Bob Lang.

MILLER

Miller's Reversible Minnow: The early model in yellow with gold spots. Varnished 700.00

Another: The later Type II in very good condition .   2,000.00

As above: Red and white with missing paint 750.0

CONDITION

Condition is all too often confused in the writing of catalogs designed to sell things. Anyone buying expensive lures (or anything else) should actually see what they are bidding on or have an agent do their bidding for them. An agent will charge a fee, but save it many times over.

MOONLIGHT

Dreadnaught: A 4" lure in red and white in original box. Excellent and rare 3,000.00

Fish Nipple: Patented in 1911, this lure comes in original box. Excellent 225.00

OSCAR PETERSON hand-carved lure is one of only several dozen known. A rare offering. Photograph by Bob Lang.

Model 1900 jointed bait: In near-mint condition 25.00

PAW PAW

Musky Hair Mouse: A 4 1/4" natural deer-hair lure with red head and black eyes. Chipped ear 125.00

Natural Hair Mouse: Red head and natural hair body. As new in box 75.00

Roman Redtail Minnow: Yellow with green head and gold spots. Rare. Very good 450.00

OSCAR PETERSON

2 5/8" lure in multicolor: By the famous fish decoy carver. Mint 1,300.00

Another: 3" in yellow & black 1,500.00

PFLUEGER

Surprise Minnow: In luminous paint. One eye is
cracked. Very good otherwise 45.00

HAIR CARE

*Lures of hair and those with feathers need special care if you hope
to keep them free of pests. A few flakes of camphor or paradichlorobenzene will do the trick.*

LOU RHEAD

Fly Rod Frog: 1 1/4" long lure has minor separation
and nose wear, but is excellent and rare 750.00

Grasshopper: 2" long in excellent condition 295.00

Darter: 3 1/4" wood, foil, and feather. Excellent 160.00

Shiner: 3 3/4" yarn, fiber, and paint. Excellent 100.00

TOM SCHROEDER

5" jointed brook trout lure: By this famous Michigan
decoy maker. Excellent 4,500.00

BROOK TROUT lure by famous Michigan decoy maker, Tom Schroeder, with a fine patina and in
near-mint condition. Photograph courtesy of Bob Lang.

SHAKESPEARE

Barnacle Bill: 2 3/4" saltwater lure with silver finish. Rare and excellent 350.00

Sea Witch saltwater lure: Spotted with glass eyes. Excellent 100.00

3-Hook Minnow: Early lure in unmarked wooden box. Good to fair 60.00

3-Hook Minnow: With "see through" wire hook hardware. Good condition 25.00

Evolution Bait: The rubber has hardened, but the lure is otherwise very good 95.00

LET THE CHIPS FALL

I was there back in time when Tom Schroeder walked off with high honors and the top prize in the last honest-to-god working decoy show ever held. My father headed that show committee, which included Joel Barber, Gene Connett, Lynn Bogue Hunt, Bill Mackay, and other notables. Schroeder and the committee have all gone now and only the wood chips and the weather remember.

BUD STEWART

3 1/2" Deep Diving Wiggler: By this fish-decoy maker. Very good condition 50.00

7" Crippled Sucker: Excellent 35.00

7 1/2" Side Sucker: Minor chipping 35.00

6 3/4" Jointed Surface Sucker: One side marred 55.00

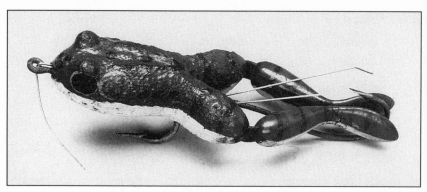

TEMPTER FROG BAIT is made of cork, has rubber legs, and is in unusually fine condition. Photograph by Bob Lang.

TEMPTER

Tempter Frog Bait: A 3 3/4" cork and rubber lure.
Weedless and near-mint condition 300.00

WAKEMAN

Archer Wakeman Skeleton Bait: Circa 1886 minnow
holding lure. Excellent 300.00

WELCH & GRAVES

Glass Minnow Tube: In part of the original
wooden box 425.00

Another: In original wooden box with the original
label. Two hooks removed 800.00

WINCHESTER

#9202 Multi-Wobbler: Glass eyes and a green, gold,
black color scheme. Near mint 300.00

#9216 Five Hook Minnow: with chips and dings 275.00

STATE DUCK STAMP PRINTS

I have followed through with the promise stated in my first *Price Guide* and herewith bring you the complete rundown on state duck stamps and duck stamp prints — subjects dear to some and abhorrent to others. Like them or not, these are sporting collectibles and deserve your attention.

It is safe to say that most state duck stamps and duck stamp prints are the result of promotion by print makers, but you must know that the first such prints — the federal stamp prints by Richard Bishop and, later, others like Roland Clark and Frank Benson — were devised, promoted, yes and pushed by Ralph Terrill and Ed Thomas of Abercrombie & Fitch's print department. I have yet to hear complaints regarding that effort, which was the beginnning of today's plethora of prints. Perhaps we have gone too far too fast and certainly *unlimited* limited editions have tended to kill the golden duck, but this is a matter between you and your print supplier. The following information can only serve as a guide. Don't let the "first of state" bug bite before you find out about limitation.

The following list begins with state duck stamp prints because these came first, even though the stamp may well have been the desired result. Without the art there could be no stamp and it is with this thought that we begin. I am indebted to Dan Coyle of Wild Wings and to the folks at The Depot in Sullivan, Illinois, for their help with this subject. The prints are listed in alphabetical order by state and then by year. Prices are for signed, mint-condition prints at retail.

ALABAMA

1979	750.00
1980	110.00
1981	110.00
1982	210.00
1983	110.00
1984	190.00
1985	110.00
1986	110.00
1987–1990	135.00

ALASKA

1985	700.00
1986	500.00
1987	210.00
1988	200.00
1989	200.00
1990	135.00

ARIZONA

1987	200.00
1988	135.00
1989	135.00
1990	145.00

ARKANSAS

1981	900.00
1982	250.00
1983	350.00
1984	300.00
1985–1987	250.00
1988	135.00

1989 . . . . 200.00
1990 . . . . 135.00

CALIFORNIA

1971 . . . . 1,750.00
1972 . . . . 2,500.00
1973–1977 . . . . 300.00
1978 . . . . 900.00
1979 . . . . 850.00
1980 . . . . 700.00
1981 . . . . 200.00
1982 . . . . 175.00
1983–1985 . . . . 150.00
1986 . . . . 190.00
1987 . . . . 200.00
1988 . . . . 135.00
1989–1990 . . . . 145.00

COLORADO

1990 . . . . 145.00

DELAWARE

1980 . . . . 800.00
1981–1989 . . . . 125.00
1990 . . . . 135.00

FLORIDA

1979 . . . . 800.00
1980–1985 . . . . 135.00
1986 . . . . 200.00
1987–1988 . . . . 135.00
1989–1990 . . . . 145.00

GEORGIA

1985	300.00
1986–1990	200.00

IDAHO

1987	200.00
1988	135.00
1989	180.00
1990	145.00

ILLINOIS

1976	4,000.00
1977–1978	500.00
1979–1980	400.00
1981	1,200.00
1982–1989	250.00
1990	135.00

INDIANA

1976	2,800.00

IOWA

1972	10,000.00
1973	700.00
1974	1,300.00
1975	200.00
1976	150.00
1977	600.00
1978	150.00
1979	900.00

1980–1982 . . . . 150.00
1983–1986 . . . . 200.00
1987–1990 . . . . 135.00

LOW NUMBERS

The $135.00 and $145.00 values for duck stamp prints are the prices at which these offerings were originally offered and if they persists ....

KANSAS

1987–1989 . . . . 135.00
1990 . . . . 300.00

KENTUCKY

1985 . . . . 350.00
1986–1988 . . . . 200.00
1989–1990 . . . . 135.00

LOUISIANA

1989 . . . . 250.00
1990 . . . . 135.00

MAINE

1984 . . . . 400.00
1985 . . . . 300.00
1986 . . . . 275.00
1987–1988 . . . . 200.00
1989 . . . . 135.00
1990 . . . . 145.00

MARYLAND

1974	6,000.00
1975	1,750.00
1976	900.00
1977	700.00
1978	300.00
1979	250.00
1980	450.00
1981	400.00
1982	300.00
1983–1985	250.00
1986–1988	200.00
1989–1990	135.00

MASSACHUSETTS

1974	1,400.00
1975	1,500.00
1976	400.00
1977	4,000.00
1978–1979	600.00
1980	350.00
1981–1982	250.00
1983	200.00
1984	400.00
1985–1987	200.00
1989–1990	140.00

MICHIGAN

1976	4,000.00
1977	1,750.00
1978	350.00
1979	500.00
1980	1,200.00
1981–1982	150.00

1983	800.00
1984	150.00
1985	275.00
1986	200.00
1987	350.00
1988	155.00
1989–1990	140.00

MINNESOTA

1977	1,800.00
1978	700.00
1979	500.00
1980	600.00
1981	150.00
1982–1985	200.00
1986	135.00
1987	275.00
1988	140.00
1989–1990	145.00

HOOSIER KNOW HOW

I recently met a man from Indianapolis who told me he owned one of the state duck stamp prints and — when I asked him which one — he told me he owned the only one. I told him he was blessed.

MISSISSIPPI

1976	3,000.00
1977	1,000.00
1978–1979	500.00
1980–1982	300.00
1983–1985	200.00

1986 . . . . 400.00
1987–1988 . . . . 150.00
1989–1990 . . . . 135.00

MISSOURI

1979 . . . . 1,750.00
1980 . . . . 250.00
1981–1982 . . . . 125.00
1983–1986 . . . . 130.00
1987–1990 . . . . 135.00

MONTANA

1978 . . . . 400.00
1979–1980 . . . . 135.00
1981–1985 . . . . none issued
1986 . . . . 275.00
1987–1990 . . . . 135.00

NEBRASKA'S 1991 STATE DUCK STAMP print, together with that from New Mexico brought the total number of states with such devices to forty-eight. Photograph courtesy of The Depot, Sullivan, Illinois.

NEBRASKA

Issued first stamp and print in 1991

NEVADA

1979	1,800.00
1980–1981	300.00
1982–1983	135.00
1984	200.00
1985	150.00
1986	135.00
1987	200.00
1988–1989	135.00
1990	145.00

NEW HAMPSHIRE

1983	600.00
1984–1985	400.00
1986	500.00
1987–1988	200.00
1989	175.00
1990	150.00

NEW JERSEY

1984	700.00
1985	500.00
1986	250.00
1987	225.00
1988	200.00
1989–1990	135.00

STATE DUCK STAMP PRINT FOR 1991 from New Mexico was one of two introduced that year. It brought the number of states that have (or have had) state duck stamp prints to forty-eight. Photograph courtesy of The Depot, Sullivan, Illinois.

NEW MEXICO

Issued first stamp and print in 1991

NEW YORK

1985–1986	275.00
1987–1988	200.00
1989	275.00
1990	135.00

NORTH CAROLINA

1983	850.00
1984	300.00
1985–1988	135.00
1989	250.00
1990	135.00

NORTH DAKOTA

1982	450.00
1983–1990	135.00

OHIO

1982	350.00
1983	300.00
1984–1988	153.00
1989–1990	175.00

OKLAHOMA

1980	750.00
1981–1988	125.00
1989	150.00
1990	135.00

OREGON

1984	350.00
1985	250.00
1986–1987	200.00
1988–1990	250.00

DUCKING THE ISSUE

I bumped into a friend of mine one afternoon while taking a break from this lengthy compilation. When I told him what I was working on, he asked me why, if there are nearly six hundred duck stamps and duck stamp prints there are fewer and fewer ducks each year? I told him I didn't know. Think about it — where does the money go?

PENNSYLVANIA

1983	1,000.00
1984	450.00
1985	200.00
1986	400.00
1987	250.00
1988–1989	200.00
1990	135.00

RHODE ISLAND

1989	200.00
1990	145.00

SOUTH CAROLINA

1981	1,600.00
1982–1983	250.00
1984–1987	200.00
1988	400.00
1989–1990	135.00

SOUTH DAKOTA

1976	2,100.00
1977	900.00
1978	400.00
1979–1985	none issued
1986	150.00
1987–1990	135.00

TENNESSEE

1979	850.00
1980	300.00

1981–1982	125.00
1983	200.00
1984	400.00
1985–1990	135.00

TEXAS

1981	900.00
1982	500.00
1983	700.00
1984	600.00
1985	125.00
1986–1987	250.00
1988	350.00
1989–1990	200.00

UTAH

1986–1987	200.00
1988–1989	135.00
1990	145.00

VERMONT

1986	250.00
1987	200.00
1988	175.00
1989–1990	135.00

VIRGINIA

1988	200.00
1989–1990	135.00

WASHINGTON

1986	275.00
1987	200.00
1988	275.00
1989	200.00
1990	135.00

WEST VIRGINIA

1987	200.00
1988–1990	135.00

WISCONSIN

1978	850.00
1979	450.00
1980	1,000.00
1981	150.00
1982	175.00
1983	200.00
1984–1990	175.00

WYOMING

1985	250.00
1986–1987	150.00
1988	135.00
1989–1990	200.00

STATE DUCK STAMPS

As I said earlier, the print preceded the stamp only because you cannot have the latter without the former. Following in that order, we move on to the subject of state duck *stamps*.

The following list is arranged alphabetically by state and then chronologically by year. I am in debt to David Boshart and his staff at National Wildlife Philatelics of Fort Myers, Florida and to Michael Jaffee of Michael Jaffee Stamps in Vancouver, Washington, who has all the answers about these things.

ALABAMA

1979	10.00
1980, 81, 82	9.00
1983, 84, 85, 86, 87	15.00
1988	12.00
1989, 90, 91	9.00

ALASKA

1985	15.00
1986	12.00
1987, 88	10.00
1989, 90, 91	9.00

ARIZONA

987 . . . . 12.00
1988 . . . . 10.00
1989, 90, 91 . . . . 9.00

ARKANSAS

1981, 82, 83 . . . . 60.00
1984 . . . . 22.00
1985, 86 . . . . 12.00
1987, 88, 89, 90, 91 . . . . 11.00

CALIFORNIA

1971 . . . . 750.00
1972 . . . . 3, 400.00
1973 . . . . 15.00
1974 . . . . 4.50
1975 . . . . 115.00
1976 . . . . 15.00
1977: $1.00 stamp 55.00
1977: $5.00 stamp 9.00
1978 . . . . 150.00
1979–1983 . . . . 7.50
1984–1991 . . . . 10.00

COLORADO

1990 . . . . 15.00
1991 . . . . 9.00

CONNECTICUT

Has no duck stamp at this writing.

DELAWARE

1980	100.00
1981	90.00
1982	95.00
1983	60.00
1984	30.00
1985	14.00
1986, 87	10.00
1988	9.00
1989, 90, 91	8.00

FLORIDA

1979	195.00
1980, 81	30.00
1982	50.00
1983	60.00
1984, 85	25.00
1986	11.00
1987, 88	7.50
1989, 90, 91	6.00

GEORGIA

1985	15.00
1986	11.00
1987–1991	8.00

HAWAII

Has no stamp at this writing.

IDAHO

1987	15.00
1988	11.00
1989, 90, 91	10.00

ILLINOIS

1975	695.00
1976	250.00
1977	195.00
1978, 79, 80, 81	115.00
(1979 error)	750.00
1982	65.00
1983	60.00
1984	55.00
1985	25.00
1986	12.00
1987, 88, 89	10.00
1990, 91	15.00

INDIANA

1976	10.00
1977–1987	8.00
1988, 89, 90, 91	10.00

IOWA

1972	175.00
1973	45.00
1974	75.00
1975	110.00
1976, 77	15.00
1978	60.00
1979	425.00

1980 .... 60.00
1981 .... 37.50
1982 .... 17.00
1983 .... 15.00
1984 .... 40.00
1985 .... 20.00
1986 .... 19.00
1987 .... 12.00
1988, 89 .... 10.00
1990 .... 9.00
1991 .... 7.50

KANSAS

1987 .... 10.00
1988 .... 6.50
1989, 90, 91 .... 6.00

KENTUCKY

1985 .... 10.00
1986–1991 .... 8.00

LOUISIANA

1989: res 11.00
    non res 13.00
1990: res 9.00
    non res 12.00
1991: res 8.50
    non res 10.00

MAINE

1984 .... 30.00

```
1985 ...............................  50.00
1986 ...............................  13.00
1987 ...............................  10.00
1988 ...............................   8.00
1989, 90, 91 .........................   5.00
```

MARYLAND

```
1974 ...............................  20.00
1975 ...............................   8.00
1976–1981 .........................   6.00
1982 ...............................   9.00
1983 ...............................  12.50
1984–1991 .........................   9.00
```

MASSACHUSETTS

```
1974 ...............................  15.00
1975–1979 .........................  10.00
1980–1987 .........................   7.50
1988, 89, 90 ........................   5.00
1991 ...............................   7.50
```

MICHIGAN

```
1976 ...............................   7.50
1977 ............................... 325.00
1978 ...............................  30.00
1979 ...............................  40.00
1980 ...............................  18.00
1981–1986 .........................  25.00
1987, 88 ...........................  12.00
1989 ...............................   7.50
1990 ...............................   6.50
1991 ...............................   6.00
```

MINNESOTA

1977	15.00
1978–1989	10.00
1990	20.00
1991	7.50

MISSISSIPPI

1976	15.00
1977–1990	10.00
1991	4.50

MISSOURI

1979	725.00
1980	150.00
1981	75.00
1982, 83, 84	50.00
1985	30.00
1986	25.00
1987	18.00
1988	11.00
1989	10.00
1990	9.00
1991	8.00

MONTANA

1986	17.50
1987	15.00
1988	13.50
1989	12.00
1990	10.00
1991	9.00

NEBRASKA

1991	10.00

NEVADA

1979	65.00
1980–1986	12.00
1987, 88	10.00
1989	6.00
1990	10.00
1991	8.00

NEW HAMPSHIRE

1983	195.00
1984	85.00
1985	85.00
1986	30.00
1987	22.00
1988	12.00
1989	11.00
1990	9.00
1991	7.00

NEW JERSEY

1984: res	55.00
non res	65.00
1985: res	19.00
non res	25.00
1986: res	12.00
non res	15.00
1987: res	10.00
non res	14.00
1988: res	8.00
non res	12.00

1989: res	6.00
non res	10.00
1990: res	5.50
non res	9.50
1991: res	4.50
non res	8.50

NEW MEXICO

1991	11.50

NEW YORK

1985	15.00
1986, 87, 88	12.00
1989	9.50
1990	8.50
1991	7.50

NORTH CAROLINA

1983	120.00
1984	55.00
1985	45.00
1986	19.00
1987	14.00
1988	12.00
1989	11.00
1990	10.00
1991	8.00

NORTH DAKOTA

1982	125.00

1983	75.00
1984	40.00
1985	30.00
1986	25.00
1987	18.00
1988	15.00
1989	12.00
1990	11.00
1991	10.00

OHIO

1982	90.00
1983, 84	85.00
1985	62.50
1986	30.00
1987	18.00
1988, 89	12.00
1990	15.00
1991	13.00

OKLAHOMA

1980	45.00
1981	35.00
1982	12.00
1983	10.00
1984	9.00
1985–1991	7.00

OREGON

1984	45.00
1985	50.00
1986	20.00

1987 . . . . 12.00
1988 . . . . 11.00
1989 . . . . 10.00
1990 . . . .   9.50
1991 . . . .   9.00

PENNSYLVANIA

1983 . . . . 35.00
1984 . . . . 25.00
1985 . . . . 14.00
1986–1989 . . . . 10.00
1990 . . . .   8.50
1991 . . . .   8.00

RHODE ISLAND

1989 . . . . 15.00
1990 . . . . 12.00
1991 . . . . 10.50

SOUTH CAROLINA

1981 . . . . 95.00
1982 . . . . 95.00
1983 . . . . 110.00
1984 . . . . 75.00
1985 . . . . 70.00
    (# on reverse) 90.00
1986 . . . . 35.00
    (# on reverse) 45.00
1987 . . . . 22.00
    (# on reverse) 25.00
1988 . . . . 30.00
    (# on reverse) 30.00

1989 . . . . 15.00
(# on reverse) 15.00
1990 . . . . 10.00
(# on reverse) 10.00
1991 . . . . 8.50

SOUTH DAKOTA

1976 . . . . 30.00
1977 . . . . 20.00
1978 . . . . 12.00
1979–1985 . . . . (none issued)
1986 . . . . 15.00
1987 . . . . 8.00
1988 . . . . 7.00
1989 . . . . 6.00
1990 . . . . 5.00
1991 . . . . 4.00

TENNESSEE

1979 res 225.00
non res 1,295.00
1980 res 75.00
non res 600.00
1981 . . . . 45.00
1982, 83 . . . . 85.00
1984 . . . . 95.00
1985 . . . . 32.50
1986 . . . . 20.00
1987 . . . . 15.00
1988 . . . . 12.00
1989 . . . . 11.00
1990 . . . . 19.00
1991 . . . . 17.00

TEXAS

1981	45.00
1982	40.00
1983	225.00
1984	30.00
1985	18.00
1986	12.00
1987	10.00
1988	9.00
1989	8.50
1990	8.00
1991	10.00

UTAH

1986	11.00
1987	8.00
1988, 89	7.00
1990	5.50
1991	5.00

VERMONT

1986	11.00
1987	10.00
1988	9.00
1989	8.00
1990	7.50
1991	7.00

VIRGINIA

1988	15.00

1989 . . . . 10.00
1990 . . . . 9.00
1991 . . . . 8.00

WASHINGTON

1986 . . . . 11.00
1987 . . . . 10.00
1988 . . . . 9.50
1989 . . . . 9.50
1990 . . . . 10.00
1991 . . . . 9.00

WEST VIRGINIA

Note: Resident and non-resident stamps were issued
    each year and are of equal value.

1987 . . . . 15.00
1988, 89, 90 . . . . 10.00
1991 . . . . 8.50

WISCONSIN

1978 . . . . 140.00
1979 . . . . 45.00
1980, 81 . . . . 15.00
1982, 83, 84 . . . .   8.00
1985, 86 . . . . 10.00
1987, 88, 89, 90 . . . .   6.00
1991 . . . .   8.50

WYOMING

1985 . . . . 9.50
Non-waterfowl issued from 1986

APPENDIX

There are hundreds of reliable dealers. Following are some I have dealt with and can recommend. I will add to these lists in subsequent editions of this book.

SPORTING ART AND PRINTS
The Bedford Sportsman: Bedford Hills, NY 10507
Collector's Choice: 10725 Equestrian Drive, Santa Ana, CA 92705
Russell A. Fink Gallery: 9843 Gunston Road, Lorton, VA 22079
Petersen Galleries: 9433 Wilshire Blvd., Beverly Hills, CA 90212
Sportsman's Edge: 136 East 74 Street, New York, NY 10021
Wild Wings: Lake City, MN 55041

SPORTING-BOOK AUCTIONS
Oinonen Book Auctions: Box 470, Sunderland, MA 01375
Swann Auction Galleries: 104 East 25 Street, New York, NY 10010

SPORTING-BOOK DEALERS
Anglers & Shooters Bookshelf: Goshen, CT 06756
Anglers Art: P.O. Box 148, Plainfield, PA 17081
Johnny Appleseed's Books: Route 7A, Manchester, VT 05254
Judith Bowman Books: Pound Ridge Road, Bedford, NY 10506
Callahan & Co.: Box 505, Peterborough, NH 03458
Connecticut River Bookshop: Goodspeed Landing, East Haddam, CT
    06423
Gary Estabrook: Box 61453, Vancouver, WA 98666
Fair Chase, Inc: P.O. Box 880, Twin Lakes, WI 53181
Fin 'N Feather Gallery: Box 13, N. Gramby, CT 06060

David Foley: 76 Bonneville Road, West Hartford, CT 06107
Game Bag Books: 2704 Ship Rock Road, Willow Street, PA 17584
Highwood Bookshop: Box 1246, Traverse City, MI 49685
Frank J. Mikesh: 1356 Walden Road, Walnut Creek, CA 94596
Pisces and Capricorn Books: 514 Linden, Albion, MI 49224
Ray Riling Arms Books: Box 18925, Philadelphia, PA 19119
Trophy Room Books: 4858 Dempsey Avenue, Encino, CA 91436

DUCK STAMPS AND DUCK-STAMP PRINTS

The Depot: Sullivan, IL 61951
Russell A. Fink Gallery: 9843 Gunston Road, Lorton, VA 22079
Michael Jaffe: Box 61484, Vancouver, WA 98666
National Wildlife Philatelics: Box 061397, Fort Myers, FL 33905
Wild Wings: Lake City, MN 55041

FISHING-TACKLE AUCTIONS

Bob Lang: Turtle Cove: Raymond, ME 04071

FISHING TACKLE AND ACCESSORIES

The American Sporting Collector: Arden Drive, Amawalk, NY 10501
Frederick Grafeld: 297 Born Street, Seacaucus, NJ 07094
Heritage Enterprises: 22A 3rd Street, Turners Falls, MA 01376
Martin J. Keane: P.O. Box 288, Ashley Falls, MA 01222
John E. Schoffner: 624 Merritt, Fife Lake, MI 49633
Woodruff's Old Corkers: Main Street, Jamaica, VT 05343

FISHING TACKLE MUSEUM

American Museum of Fly Fishing: Route 7A, Manchester, VT 05254

DECOY AUCTIONS

Richard A. Bourne Co., Inc.: P.O. Box 141, Hyannisport, MA 02647

Ted Harmon: 2320 Main Street, West Barnstable, MA 02668
Gary Guyette-Frank Schmidt Inc.: Box 522, West Farmington, ME
    04992

DECOY DEALERS
Henry Fleckenstein: Box 577, Cambridge, MD 21613
RJG Antiques: P.O. Box 2033, Hampton, NH 03842

SPORTING FIREARMS
W. M. Bryan & Co.: P.O. Box 12492, Raleigh, NC 27605
Cape Outfitters: Route 3, Box 437, Cape Girardeau, MO 63701
Chadick's Ltd.: Box 100, Terrell, TX 75160
Michael de Chevrieux: P.O. Box 1182, Hailey, ID 83333
Griffin & Howe: 33 Claremont Road, Bernardsville, NJ 07924
New England Arms Co.: Kittery Point, ME 03905

SHOOTING ACCESSORIES
Circus Promotions: 614 Cypruswood Drive, Spring, TX 77388
James Tillinghast: P.O. Box 19-C, Hancock, NH 03449

SPORTING ADVERTISING
Circus Promotions: 614 Cypruswood Drive, Spring, TX 77388
Robert P. Hanafee: 29 Bedford Court, Amherst, MA 01002

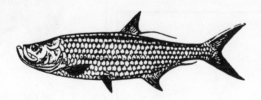

JUDITH BOWMAN BOOKS

WE MAINTAIN A HUGE INVENTORY
OF
RARE AND OUT-OF-PRINT
BOOKS AND EPHEMERA
ON

ANGLING
-
HUNTING
-
RELATED NATURAL HISTORY
-
GUNS AND DOGS
-
OLD TACKLE AND GUN CATALOGS
-
IF WE DON'T HAVE IT IN STOCK
WE'LL SEARCH FOR IT
TRY US!

TWO LARGE CATALOGS ISSUED YEARLY SINCE 1980
$5.00 PUTS YOU ON THE MAILING LIST
-
LIBRARY DEVELOPMENT AND APPRAISALS
-
WE BUY BOOKS TOO!
SINGLE VOLUMES, YOUR DUPLICATES OR YOUR WHOLE LIBRARY

Pound Ridge Road
Bedford, NY 10506
(914) 234-7543
Judith and Jim Bowman
Open by Appointment Only

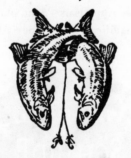
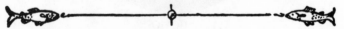